Praise for *Raising Kids*

"Through a richly relational lens, and using powerful yet simple principles, *Raising Kids* offers clear, unambivalent strategies that get results in the moment. This book is a must-have for parents who aim to raise grounded, mind- and heart-ful children who will have the skills, tools, and confidence they need to navigate the world."
—Petra H. Steinbuchel, MD, child and adolescent psychiatrist and director, UC San Francisco Child & Adolescent Psychiatry Portal

"In direct and unfluffy prose, *Raising Kids* provides the rationale as well as the language to use to support children through everyday difficulties. Informed by decades of work with children and families in clinical practice and in schools, the authors show us how to engage in helpful ways with children's feelings as they ebb and flow. In today's climate of intensive parenting, *Raising Kids* offers indispensable guidance and welcome relief."
—Diana Divecha, PhD, assistant clinical professor, Yale Child Study Center

"*Rasing Kids* is warm and relatable and sensible—all things parents need in a parenting book. Rather than providing prescriptions, *Raising Kids* helps parents understand themselves better, so that they can respond to any challenging parenting situation with confidence, awareness, and integrity. This holistic approach to parenting is much needed, and truly spot on!"
—Susan Eva Porter, LCSW, adolescent psychotherapist and author of *Bully Nation: Why America's Approach to Childhood Aggression is Bad for Everyone*

"As a physician, I know *Raising Kids* will enter my must-have parenting resources not only because of its accessible '*how-to*' approach, but also because it addresses '*why*.' The authors show you how to get on the same side as your kids, find your values 'spot,' and gain tools for getting back on track when you find yourself struggling. An exceptional parenting resource for the 21st century—it's about time!"
—Catherine Sonquist Forest, MD, MPH, former medical director and clinical associate professor, Stanford University School of Medicine

"The authors successfully blend their experience with anecdotes and practical lessons on how to raise resilient children while maintaining one's perspective—or sanity, in some cases—leaving the reader hopeful rather than powerless in striking balance and setting limits. As an educator, I plan to disseminate the lessons learned from the book. As a parent, I will rethink and re-shape some of the misconceptions and fears that I brought to parenting my two children. *Raising Kids* is an essential read for parents who want to parent with purpose, integrity, and equanimity."
—Percy L. Abram, PhD, head of school at The Bush School (WA)

Raising Kids

Raising Kids

YOUR ESSENTIAL GUIDE TO EVERYDAY PARENTING

Sheri Glucoft Wong, LCSW, and
Olaf Jorgenson, EdD

Matt Holt Books
An Imprint of BenBella Books, Inc.
Dallas, TX

Raising Kids copyright © 2022 by Sheri Glucoft Wong

Matt Holt is an imprint of BenBella Books, Inc.
10440 N. Central Expressway
Suite 800
Dallas, TX 75231
benbellabooks.com
Send feedback to feedback@benbellabooks.com

BenBella and *Matt Holt* are federally registered trademarks.

Printed in the United States of America
10 9 8 7 6 5 4 3 2 1

Library of Congress Control Number: 2022015509
ISBN 9781637743232 (trade paperback)
ISBN 9781637743249 (electronic)

Copyediting by Karen Wise
Proofreading by Madeline Grigg and Kellie Doherty
Indexing by Wordco
Text design and composition by PerfecType, Nashville, TN
Cover design by Brigid Pearson
Printed by Lake Book Manufacturing

Special discounts for bulk sales are available. Please contact bulkorders@benbellabooks.com.

I dedicate this book to all of the children in my life, who have been my true mentors; and most especially to my daughters, Jamie and Jessie, who have kept me learning, laughing, growing, and forever grateful to be their mom.

SGW

Raising Kids is dedicated to the memory of my devoted parents, Barney and Rosemarie, to my beloved wife and parenting partner, Tanya, and to our daughter, Juliette, who widened our world and filled it with wonder.

OJ

Contents

Foreword

Who among us hasn't longed for a "do-over" with some aspect of our parenting? I know I have. Let me put it to you plainly: I have had the privilege of a good deal of education and am the author of a well-regarded parenting book that was based on my experiences as a university dean. Yet when it came to raising my son and daughter, I found it hard to step into my authority as a parent.

For example, I didn't know how to set boundaries or expectations with my kids without coming off as "mean." I searched for a compromise in every single transition or tough moment because I wanted to minimize hard feelings and hoped every decision would feel fair. I felt a great deal of stress whenever my kid's perspective conflicted with mine or when the kids experienced any type of conflict with one another. In the aggregate, this amounted to me shirking my authority until I reached a boiling point, at which point I felt unappreciated as a parent and got frustrated or downright angry.

In hindsight, I can see that I didn't fully appreciate how a child steadily grows from the utter dependency of earliest childhood into a fully capable adult. Or of how a parent either facilitates or hinders that growth. I also didn't know that my ability to regulate *my* actions and reactions would set the context for my children's upbringing, for my effectiveness as their parent, and for how it would *feel* to be a member of our family.

Oh, how I wish I'd had this book to guide me. In its pages, authors Sheri Glucoft Wong (an esteemed San Francisco Bay Area family therapist, consultant, and parent educator) and Dr. Olaf "Ole" Jorgenson (a Silicon Valley–based school leader, trainer, and teacher) offer a guided hands-on approach that I found myself quoting well before the book was published. As an author and speaker in the parenting space, I have the opportunity to read and support many of the new titles published each year. Trust me when I say that *Raising Kids* is in a different league, and that our parenting bookshelves will be enhanced by its presence.

I met Ole while drafting my own book *How to Raise an Adult*. The idea for my book came from the overparenting I'd observed as a college dean and experienced as a parent in Silicon Valley, but I wanted to know if K–12 educators could support my hunch that overparenting harms kids. A friend put me in touch with Ole, the longtime head of school at Almaden Country Day School (ACDS), which is an independent school for pre-K–eighth graders in San Jose, California, that offers "a unique balance of academic rigor, character development, and the joy of childhood." Needless to say, Ole had indeed witnessed parents struggling with overparenting in his school community, and it's fair to say that he was as concerned as I was about parents needing perspective.

Ole contributed two key examples to *How to Raise an Adult*. The first was from the ACDS preschool, where parents of a toddler who'd been hit with a plastic shovel in the sandbox by another toddler wanted something to be done about the "bully." The second was from his upper school, where parents of sixth graders wanted to come along on the kids' overnight trip "just in case." Ole found both examples concerning. In the case of the sandbox, he told me that it's sad but developmentally normal and true that preschoolers will sometimes hit each other. While the child on the receiving end is understandably upset and perhaps a tad hurt, when adults provide empathy and express confidence in the child's resilience, it empowers that child to manage subsequent difficult moments. Meanwhile, the shovel-wielder needs to be talked with about how hitting hurts people, and to learn how to express feelings using their words, not be punished for being a "bully."

In the case of the overnight trip, he said the very purpose of such an outing in middle school is to give kids a chance to be away from home and family, and to expand their learning and coping horizons by getting them out of their comfort zone. A parent's presence doesn't let children stretch into that independence. Taken as a whole, the through line is a parent's understanding about what's developmentally appropriate for a child, about how children develop competence and confidence, and about when a parent should intervene and how.

After six years of quoting Ole's perspective, I was delighted to hear that he and Sheri were teaming up to write a parenting book. Sheri had supported parents at ACDS for years; Ole persuaded her to expand their collaboration and coauthor a book. Ole brought his educational background and writing experience to capture the effective parenting insights, anecdotes, tips, and language that have marked Sheri's career as a therapist and speaker. This book is the result: a guide parents can use whenever we need help getting "on our spot."

With decades of experience counseling families and teaching kids, having raised children of their own, and bringing a mindful eye to how parenting has changed in recent decades, their book makes a significant contribution to the growing body of literature that suggests that getting clear on what's going on for *us* as parents makes all the difference in the lives of our children.

When parents aren't able to distinguish between our child's activities and experiences and our own, when we hesitate to set clear boundaries and expectations with our children, and when we're reluctant to let our children experience disappointment, we contribute to the skills deficits and mental health challenges so many kids experience today. In Sheri and Ole's words, "The process of learning how to handle disappointment is essential to becoming a resilient, confident, and happy person, and the job of teaching resilience belongs primarily to parents." We do this by knowing how to find and stay on our "spot" as parents, including how we relate to our kids interpersonally, set boundaries, encourage manners, instill values, and set limits.

We are on our "spot" when we are self-regulated in mind, heart, and body, instead of hemming and hawing on the one hand or being overly controlling on the other. When we're anxious about our kids' fears, experiences, and outcomes to such an extent that we over-involve ourselves in those things, we've left our "spot" and get in the way of our kids finding their own "spots."

The book's fundamental premise is one I wholeheartedly endorse: We are not our child. We have our spot and they have theirs. When we stay on our spot as parents, we create an unconditionally loving relationship that fosters loads of autonomy in our kids. Our kids then develop agency, resilience, skills, strength, emotional wellness, *and* a stronger relationship with us. Doesn't that sound amazing?

Or does it sound daunting? As Sheri and Ole have reminded me, "You were able to let go of the bike seat because you understood that although they might fall, you couldn't give them balance or courage, and they were going to have to take some risks to conquer the bike themselves. Once they did, they could peddle off with self-assurance." The scenarios and dialogues that Sheri and Ole provide, just like this one, are precisely the guidance we need in the many, many moments that constitute "parenting." Of all that is in this marvelously instructive book, the greatest and most reassuring advice Sheri and Ole offer is that it's never too late: "No matter how old your kids are," they say, "you can find your spot at any time and begin to relate from there." I know you're counting on this to be true as much as I am.

Julie Lythcott-Haims
Palo Alto, California

Introduction

It was an exasperating, awful Thursday night, and Tyler's parents were overwhelmed. They felt exhausted from arguing with their son. Nothing they tried had worked, and the situation was deteriorating.

Tyler, age nine, had been yelling at his brother all evening and was unwilling to clean up the mess he'd left on the kitchen table. He refused to take a bath, and he grew more combative and rude to his parents as the night wore on. They tried every approach they could think of to convince him to cooperate and start getting ready for bedtime, now hours overdue.

Tyler's dad was determined that Tyler clean up his mess; Tyler's mom demanded an apology for speaking rudely. Their insistence and frustration only made Tyler more stubborn, and his contentious behavior worsened. Nothing was working, they grew increasingly agitated and desperate, and it was getting late.

As she was about to approach Tyler and enter into another round of the same power struggle, Tyler's mom paused and took a deep breath. She had attended one of Sheri's parenting workshops the week before at her children's school, and she had taken notes on points that resonated. She looked at her notes:

"When several issues come up at once, you can address only one at a time. Ask yourself, what matters most to you in this moment?"

Tyler's mom realized that above all, it was way past Tyler's bedtime and he was exhausted. She knew what mattered most was that Tyler get to sleep.

1

But what about the rudeness and the apology he owed, as well as the mess he wouldn't clean up? She looked at her notes again:

"Once you are clear about what matters most, focus on just that, knowing you can address other issues at a different time."

Tyler's mom knew they needed to attend to his out-of-bounds behavior, but she also realized that trying to solve issues with an overly tired and frustrated kid wouldn't work. They needed to stay focused on getting Tyler to bed, which itself was going to be a challenge since they were tired and frustrated, too. She went back to her notes:

"As frustrated as we may feel, remembering that we love our kids and they love us softens the rough times for everyone."

She went into Tyler's room, where he was half-heartedly playing with his building set. She took a deep breath and said, "It's late, sweetheart, and time to put pajamas on and get into bed. We've been having a rough time, but sometimes that happens, and we always work it out. We'll work this one out, too . . . tomorrow. Come on, I'll help you."

Tyler glared at his mom, who almost lost her resolve as a result of his look, but she was clear and able to stay with what mattered most, and that was making sure Tyler went to bed.

With her conviction and gentle resolve, she eased Tyler into his pajamas and tucked him in. She knew they'd all be more reasonable the next day, when they could talk as a family about better ways to relate and to avoid these power struggles.

There's No One Way to Raise Kids

Most of us have had a Thursday night like Tyler's parents did. In the midst of these emotional moments, we need to find a way to interact with our children that fits our priorities, values, instincts, and, most importantly, our relationship with our kids.

Ultimately, when it comes to parenting, there are no "one-size-fits-all" solutions. Formulaic parenting methods and techniques don't take into account the innumerable ways to be a parent (or to be a child!). No single approach applies to the range of cultures, lifestyles, forms, and dynamics of today's families, nor to the wide variation in the ways children learn, relate, identify, and look for their place in the world.

Parents, families, and children are simply too richly diverse for standardized templates or prescriptions. When parents try to implement techniques that don't have a basis in who they are, what they value, and how they relate to their kids, they often feel forced and ineffective when their children don't respond as expected. This is because *parenting approaches only work when they are supported by the relationships parents have with their kids.*

This is the main reason we wrote this book. *Raising Kids* helps you integrate who you are, what you know about yourself and your children, and what matters most to you as parents, with the steps for you to teach and guide your kids. We'll show you approaches that let you be on your children's side even as you take on the leadership roles of taskmaster, limit-setter, and family guide that are essential and often daunting aspects of everyday parenting.

Raising Kids is meant to be there for you when you need to summon your best parenting self during daily life with children. We chose "daily life" because how we relate to our children day to day forms their sense of themselves, their connection to us, and their ways of being in the world. No interaction we have with our children is too small to strengthen our relationship, to impart our values, to build their confidence, and to demonstrate communicating, relating, and caring.

We also chose to focus this book on daily life because home is the training ground for how to be in the world. Our kids' perspectives and expectations about life beyond their household are shaped by daily life in their family. How we manage everyday life—including setbacks and conflicts—helps prepare children for the bigger, weightier issues they're bound to encounter after they leave home.

A Book That Includes What Parents Have Taught *Us*

Raising Kids captures what we've seen that *works* with parents and children across decades of experience, and is supported by feedback parents shared with us as their kids have grown. We are a uniquely qualified writing team: a San Francisco Bay Area family therapist and a Silicon Valley private school head. Between us, we've spent more than eight decades helping parents manage the inevitable challenges of raising children as they grow up, navigate setbacks and changes, and prepare to thrive in the world outside the home.

What we bring to this book goes far beyond our professional training. It includes what we've learned from the many parents and children we've worked with over the years. Parents have relayed to us what specific advice truly helped them relate more harmoniously and effectively. Our approaches are affirmed by extensive research and our own training, but the select guidance we share in this book emerged from decades of real-life, firsthand interactions with parents, children, and families.

These approaches have already worked for thousands of parents, teachers, caregivers, and children. They have been shared over the past forty years with audiences at Stanford, Yale, UC Berkeley, UC San Francisco, and in hundreds of schools, school districts, preschools, daycare centers, businesses, medical centers, and after-school programs around the country.

This book is an anthology of proven guidance focused on relationship-building that can be adapted to virtually any family structure or dynamic, with children ages two to twenty and beyond—because it's never too late to create the relationship you want with your kids.

A Guide for Everyday Life with Kids

Whether or not kids or parents have special challenges, whether or not your family life or situation are typical, whether you're on your own or partnered—whatever your circumstances are, there are universals in everyday life with children that send all parents looking for perspective, tools, and support. This book is not intended to be a substitute for the help of a counselor, health provider, or learning specialist when professional involvement is needed. Rather, it was written to take that everyday walk along with you as you navigate these universal aspects of daily parenting.

- We'll offer approaches and language you can use when you feel at a loss with your children, as Tyler's parents did.

- We'll help you figure out when to engage with a difficult situation and when to step back.

- We'll support you in gaining a clearer sense of what matters to you as a parent and how to communicate that in a way that your kids will hear.

- We'll show you how common parenting assumptions may actually be part of the problem you're experiencing.

- We'll share ways to build your parenting confidence and effectiveness and improve your relationships with your children.

Raising Kids is intended to help you when you're feeling overwhelmed and ineffective as a parent (or "off your spot," as we call it) and when you need a little help to get back on track. We focus on helping you parent your children in a way that puts you both on the same side, with your relationship firmly at the center of your everyday life.

We offer tools and techniques that you can apply to everyday parenting situations, which in turn will help you enjoy your kids even more. After all, isn't that the whole point of being a parent?

How This Book Is Different—and Why It Matters

Raising Kids isn't a typical parenting book.

- **We focus on what's working, not what's "wrong."** Our advice addresses parents where they are, not where they "should be." We've learned that in the midst of feeling overwhelmed and ineffective, parents lose sight of the fact that at least some of what they do with their kids really does work. We help parents identify and better understand what they're doing *right* so that they can build on that. When parents recognize the confidence and conviction they already have in those aspects of parenting where they feel successful, they can better apply our approaches to areas where they struggle.

- **We put parents and kids on the same side.** It's tempting for parents to seek tactics to help them regain control over their children's unwanted behaviors. This way of thinking casts children as adversaries who have to be outwitted or outwilled for parents to manage them. We approach this from a different angle: We assume that children are bound to make missteps and push boundaries as they figure out how to be in the world; they're just trying to figure out how the world works, and they look to their parents for guidance. Rather than feeling like parents have to control children, instead we emphasize words and actions that help kids *understand*. This allows parents and children to be on the same side.

- **We provide the why, not just the what.** We set out to explain what makes the approaches effective so that you can understand, internalize, and apply them when you need them. Our book is not simply about following a formula for managing misbehaving kids; it's about understanding your interactions with your children and showing you how to turn your confident, effective parenting moments into a consistent pattern that strengthens your relationship with your children.

Finding Your Spot: Where Authentic and Effective Parenting Begins

Your spot is that place inside you where reasoning, loving, intuition, and conviction come together as you make a decision. When you're on your spot, you are fully present and confident as you relate to your kids. In other words, your spot is the place you come from where you're resolved and certain, and your kids can sense the caring, clarity, and confidence in your communications with them. When you're on your spot, you truly connect with your children; they sense it and respond to that connection.

Starting in our first chapter, this book is designed to help parents learn how to find their spot and stay on it. We'll help you take the parenting roles and practices that already work well for you and bring that same clarity and conviction to the areas where you feel less effective. Parents who find their spot gain access to perspective and confidence, transforming even the most challenging parenting moments into interactions that support relationships with your kids.

A Parenting Guide by Your Side

Parents today lead full, hectic lives. We know that for a parenting resource to be helpful, it must be user friendly and easy to internalize, and it must provide practical coaching. *Raising Kids* helps you find your spot on a wide range of parenting topics. At the end of the chapters, we include a handful of "Spotlights"—considerations and action steps to help you put the book to use in your everyday parenting.

A few Spotlights from the chapters include the following:

- To have true self-esteem, kids need to know two things: that they're unique and special and that they're just like everyone else.

- Setting limits is a loving act; "no" is part of a balanced developmental diet.

- Be curious, not furious; children's behavior makes more sense when you know the rest of the story.

You can also use the Spotlights as prompts when you find yourself in unexpected or challenging parenting territory—which for most parents is often!

We begin the book with what we hope will become your starting place, too: finding your spot.

Finding Your "Spot"

In good times and hard times, family life can feel like a three-ring circus. The constant juggling of household, work, and raising kids can throw you off-balance so you end up spending more time regaining control than building the relationships you want to have with your children.

In the midst of fatigue and frazzle, you may find yourself becoming dismissive, emotional, or overreactive with your kids, losing sight of how you're responding to the people you love most in the world. In those moments, you are literally "beside yourself." You're off your spot.

But there are also times when you're on your spot and fully aware of your parenting self. This is when each part is operating in concert:

- Your **head** (your decision follows your good judgment)
- Your **heart** (it comes from a loving place inside you)
- Your **gut** (your instincts tell you it's right)
- Down to your **feet** (you are ready to stand firm and walk your talk)

You feel confident, resolved, and ready to take action steps. You're tuned in, grounded, and clear—and your children sense it.

This is being "on your spot," and it is key to effective parenting.

Seat Belts

Think about those areas of family life that are ongoing challenges for you: morning routine, mealtime, clean-up, homework, screen time, bedtime. When parents become exasperated, it's pretty common to fall into cycles with their kids—pushing back, avoiding the problems, nagging, and arguing.

Ask yourself: Do you have to work that hard to get your kids to wear their seat belts in the car?

Most parents tell us they don't have to struggle with children about seat belts (or car seats). When asked, "Why not?" they usually respond, "Because it's so important; it's a matter of safety, and it's nonnegotiable," as if their kids somehow just know that.

The truth is, your success with seat belts demonstrates your capacity for effective parenting. Although you may struggle in other areas, you can count on your kids to buckle up without a fuss. And there's a reason for that!

Typically, parents hold a highly protective and unwavering conviction about wearing seat belts, even if it initially requires some persistence in the face of protests or kicking seats. Actually, the same is true when it comes to keeping your children from running in the street, playing near a hot stove, or a host of other unquestionable dangers. Like seat belts, these are safety issues, so parents have clarity about their expectations and limits; it feels wise and loving for you to insist on seat belts, with no exceptions.

And as a result, children cooperate because they perceive your combined clarity, certainty, and heart. *This is what happens when you are on your spot.*

How can you bring this sense of conviction you have toward seat belts to areas of parenting where you feel less effective? In other words, how can you find your spot, know it, and show your kids that you're on it, as you do with seat belts?

When you want to get your child on board in other areas, ask yourself whether it's an issue about which you can summon the same clarity and commitment that you do about seat belts. Are you as clear and resolved about what needs to happen, from head to toe—your judgment is sure, your heart is in it, your instincts align, and you're ready to hold your ground?

If so, this is a "seat belt issue" for you. You can get on your spot to address it. If not—if you don't have that head-to-toe clarity and resolve—then let it go for now.

Bella was six years old, and her sister Sonia was eight. Their dad loved to walk with them to their neighborhood breakfast place on the weekends. The problem was that—as with their mealtime experience at home—the girls' behavior at the restaurant quickly became silly and then quarrelsome. They grew progressively louder, which was disruptive and stressful for their dad, and even more unpleasant for the other patrons and waitstaff.

Their dad tried bribing, threatening, nagging, and cajoling them, but by the end of breakfast, their behavior was often beyond his control.

When Sheri asked him how the walk to the restaurant went each time, the girls' dad looked perplexed. "The walk is always fine," he replied.

"You mean the kids stay on the sidewalk, no tripping each other or running off?"

"Of course not!" their dad replied assuredly. "I make sure they're good about safety."

Undoubtedly, the girls were getting clear messages about their behavior on the sidewalk when they needed to be safe. If their dad were as clear and "on his spot" about restaurant manners as he was about safety on the walk there, their time together at breakfast would likely be very different. So "safety" was a priority for him, but he hadn't made restaurant behavior a seat belt issue—yet.

What Is Your Spot?

Your spot is where you stand when you feel confident, clear, and committed to making a decision, holding the line, and following through. You're on your spot when you know what you want to happen, your heart is in it, your gut says it's right, and you are resolved to make it happen.

But your spot is more than resolve and conviction. While being on your spot may be most visible when you're managing emotions and behaviors, setting limits, or enlisting your child's cooperation, you also want to be on your spot when you are comforting, advising, or inspiring your child. You find that place inside where your head, heart, and instincts combine so that you can support your child with understanding, clarity, and confidence.

All parents have spots that they are able to hold, in the moment or consistently. When you are setting limits and use the time-tested countdown to get your kids to cooperate ("One . . . two . . . THREE"), they typically will come around before you get to three. "THREE" signals your limit; you know it and they know it.

This familiar tactic is actually a countdown to your spot. You're giving the message that whatever's going on, it isn't getting past "three." If you fake this, overuse it, keep going past three, start over, or are unclear about what happens after the countdown, you aren't on your spot, your kids know it, and it doesn't work.

But the truth is, you don't need a countdown to get to your spot. When you wait to pour the apple juice until you hear "please," when you ride out the tears and insist that screen time really is over, when you aim a no-nonsense look at your kid who is interrupting your conversation and she stops to wait her turn, then you are on your spot. These are not just techniques for managing behavior; they are extensions of your relationship with your child.

There are lots of reasons parents are unable to get on their spot. You may be sympathetic to a kid who wants to linger in bed in the morning and then find yourself nagging him to hurry through each step of getting dressed and eating breakfast. You have a picture of how you'd like the morning to go, but in your ambivalence about insisting versus indulging, you can lack the clear conviction that would put you in charge of making it happen in the way you imagine. What started off as caring sympathy can unintentionally end up creating conflict and upset.

Similarly, you might stray from your spot because of guilt: "I've been at work all day, and it's hard to make my child go to bed when she wants more time with me." You may also get off your spot when you over-identify with your child: "I get bored easily, too; I understand why she's up and down from the table." Sometimes you move from your spot out of confusion: "Maybe I need to let her be rude to me sometimes so she can develop her independence."

You'll have trouble staying on your spot if you are unsure in your head, heart, or gut and you're unprepared to follow through with action. In this case, it's best to stop and figure out why you aren't clear on a decision, or why you can't take steps to address a situation that bothers you. For instance, if it's important to you that your child goes to bed at a certain time, what stops you from standing behind that priority when it isn't happening?

Here are two examples of how parents struggle to get on their spot about bedtime:

> You want your teenager in bed by 10 PM, but she still has homework. This is an ongoing issue that you've pressed and met resistance. She procrastinates about getting started, gets distracted by texts and social media, and then she doesn't finish by bedtime. You want her homework to be complete, but you're frustrated that she isn't getting the rest she needs and then has a hard time getting up the next day. She's a conscientious student and you want to support that, so it's tough to insist on her bedtime. This is a dilemma, and you haven't found your spot; consequently, you've given your daughter mixed bedtime messages.

• • •

> You put your young child to bed and say good night, and in a few minutes, he calls out that he's hungry or thirsty or that you forgot to hug him. You

want him to be comfortable and to feel loved, so you go in, perhaps several times in response to different requests. It turns out that although you declared bedtime, you aren't on your spot. You intended lights-out to mean interactions are over for the night, but you didn't have the heart to stick with it. You child has gotten the message that bedtime isn't a seat belt, and he's exploring his options.

When you're on your spot, you are actually on your children's side; you're helping them accept that the evening is over when you say good night. You know that this is good for them because they need their sleep, and it's good for you because you need your own pre-bedtime space; meeting your own needs makes you more able to meet theirs. You've gotten clear on this and following through on lights-out isn't antagonistic; it's done out of your love and caring. To stay on your spot, you need to really mean it.

If you don't mean it, or you're not willing to hold your ground, then you aren't really on your spot. Either your child needs to shut down her screen at a certain time or she doesn't. If she does, then you need to be ready to go through whatever pushback there is when you commit to being consistent about enforcing the expectation. This could entail living through a number of challenging evenings and weekends until your child accepts that you mean it. If you are firmly on your spot, the investment is worth it to you to get your kid solidly on track and in a better routine. If you aren't ready to insist on it, if you aren't quite on your spot yet, acknowledge that and let it go for now.

It's important to note that being on your spot doesn't mean being rigid; to the contrary, rigidity signals that you really aren't on your spot. Being on your spot simply means being clear, from head to toe, about where you stand and what needs to happen. Because being on your spot goes beyond taking a position—you're firm but connected to the caring behind your position—it is not dogmatic or unyielding. Your positions may shift with different situations, or different kids or different times, and when it does, you stay aligned and remain sure and confident in that shift. When you're clear from head to toe, it's easy to explain the change to your children.

On-Your-Spot Dialogue

Here are some examples around issues of daily life that illustrate the difference between being on your spot and not.

Clean-up Time

When you're announcing clean-up time:

Off your spot (in an anxious tone): *"Can you kids start cleaning up now?"* While you may think you're modeling a polite approach, this comes across to your kids as a suggestion rather than a request, as if you're inviting your children to make that decision. Your heart may not quite be in this interruption of the playtime—or your feet, either. If it isn't necessary to clean up, don't bring it up yet. Wait until you are on your spot.

On your spot (in a matter-of-fact and definitive tone): *"It's clean-up time now."* This conveys clarity that it's time to clean up. A parent who is clear from head to toe about this will follow up by going into the room to make sure that saying leads to doing, and so his children learn that he really means what he says.

When No Means No

If your child persists in asking about something you've said no to already:

Off your spot (in a defensive tone): *"Yes, but . . ."* You answer each argument your child presents with a counterargument, you defend each accusation, you correct each questionable assertion with a fact, or you try to get your child to accept your response without being angry at you. You think you're holding the line, but when parents are on their spot, they don't feel the need to engage in debate or negotiation. They are so clear that they don't need to justify, convince, or pacify, which only leads to litigation, since those approaches make your child think a case is being tried rather than that you're setting a limit.

On your spot (in a kind yet firm tone): *"My answer about this is no, and that is not going to change. If you want to talk about this, we can talk now* [or name another time when you are willing to have a conversation], *although it won't change my decision this time."*

A child who really wants to be heard and understood will take you up on that invitation to talk. A child who is just hoping to shake your conviction in the moment probably won't. Either way, you've been clear that you stand firm.

Refusing to Do Homework

When your child refuses to cooperate in general:

Off your spot (in a threatening tone): *"If you don't do your homework, then you can't go to the sleepover tomorrow"* (or play your video game, or have a friend over, and so forth). This might feel like you're on your spot since you are clear about what is required. But threatening your children conveys that you're not sure you have the authority to insist on it. You may follow through, but the fact that you're invoking threats sounds (and is) less grounded and more desperate, a sign to your kids that you're off your spot, and no longer on the same side with them.

On your spot (in a matter-of-fact, this-is-how-it-works tone): *"When your homework is finished, then you'll be set to go to the sleepover"* or *"When your homework is done, then you can play your video game"* (or have your friend over, and so on).

Declaring "when" rather than "if" may seem like a subtle difference, but it's an important one and it will register much differently with your child. When you're on your spot about how things work in your family, you are able to communicate the sequencing with conviction: When the have-tos are done, then the want-tos get to happen. You don't need to use leverage or to threaten with "and if you don't . . ." While your children may push back or probe to see if things really do work this way, when you stay on your spot and follow through with the boundaries you've established, then your kids will learn to accept your when-thens with the same matter-of-fact spirit that you have about holding to them.

Finding Your Spot

When a day-to-day issue becomes a struggle, the first step (in a calm moment) is to pause and reflect. Check your own resolve, and be honest with yourself. If you're not clear about what you want and why, it will come across in vague communication and inconsistent messages. You may start out with a conciliatory or bargaining tone and end up impatient. Your ambiguity is confusing, so you're less likely to be understood and get cooperation, and you're more likely to encounter resistance, argument, and distress as your child tries to figure out where you really stand.

When you're off your spot, you're less grounded, less clear, and often less able to remain kind. Rather than being firm, you may become harsh. In those exasperated moments (we've all had them, and we regret them), we may forget to communicate like family members who love each other. That's why it's really worth taking the time to find your spot first. Step back, remove yourself for a few minutes if you can, take a deep breath, and look for your spot using the head-to-toe checklist below.

Getting on Your Spot: The Head-to-Toe Checklist

For those moments when you can use some help finding your spot, ask yourself these questions. If the answers are yes, then the situation or behavior you're weighing is a seat belt issue for you, and you'll be able to stay on your spot. If any of the answers are no, then let it go for now, until you find your spot.

- **Head**: Does my good judgment tell me that what I want here is important and right in this moment and/or in the big picture? Is my child capable of what I am asking?

- **Heart**: Is this a loving thing to do? Do I have the heart to stand firm?

- **Gut**: Do my instincts tell me that this feels right?

- **Feet**: Am I willing to walk my talk, to take action and stand behind what it takes (with a firm but kind manner) to make this happen even in the face of tears or pushback? Can I support it consistently as needed?

All of us have areas where parenting is challenging for us, and we all have areas where we feel effective—where our children are responsive and cooperative. On those issues where you are totally clear (inside) and firmly consistent (outside), from head to toe, your kids get it and comply without the need for raised voices, nagging, or threats. Like "buckle your seat belt," it just happens. You're on your spot.

And there may be particular interactions or situations that are so upsetting and so persistent that taking a moment and running the checklist isn't enough for either or both parents. In these moments, you may want to reach out and consult a trusted advisor, wise friend, or professional counselor for clarity. Sometimes getting support, including coping strategies, is necessary to help you find your spot and get on a better track with yourself and your family.

Why Do You Need to Stay on Your Spot?

Most parents feel confident and effective about the parenting expectations and scenarios that are clear and nonnegotiable to them. Children rarely argue with parents who are on their spot, and when they do, kids quickly discover that the issue is nonnegotiable. When you are on your spot, your children get it and get with it.

In much the same way that children recognize and accept the authority of teachers or coaches who make it clear what's required and what's optional, kids understand when you demonstrate conviction. Working parents who need to be on the job at a particular time in the morning tend to have morning routines that effectively get everyone ready on time. Parents who hold and convey clear, strong values about family dinners and manners find their children honoring dinnertime and participating with courtesy (well, mostly!).

Staying on your spot shows your children what is truly important to you about day-to-day routines, how you all relate to one another, and what it means to you to be a family.

Ways to Be on Your Spot

You want to be on your spot when you communicate your values, make decisions, and set limits, or when you must disappoint your child. *Staying on your spot with your children is always about being on their side,* even if they don't see it in the moment.

Realizing this will help you enormously in those situations where parenting is really, really hard. When you have to restrict your child from an activity or insist on one for her own good, share unhappy news, or pull a dirty Band-Aid off her arm, she feels bad, and that hurts you, too. Being on your kid's side doesn't always mean agreeing with her, complimenting her, or comforting her. Sometimes it means disappointing her, thwarting her, or letting her vent or work through her feelings on her own. Remember that even though it might not seem that way to your child, when you are on your spot, you are on her side.

Staying on your spot also means remembering that you love this person, even when you are upset. We all get to that place when we are "beside ourselves"—we're off our spot. We sometimes have to remind ourselves that the person we're upset with is someone we love deeply and want to help, and then we can find our way back to our caring spot, the very same caring spot we're on when we let our kids know it's time to buckle up.

Flexible Parenting: Adjusting Your Spot as You Move with Life's Changes

Just as being firm doesn't mean being rigid, staying on your spot doesn't mean your position is always static. Your stance or course of action in a given moment may need to shift based on your child's development, new circumstances, or changing needs. As reasonable requests or unexpected situations present themselves, you want to be responsive. These and other variables that are just part of life may call for parents to adjust their approaches. Being on your spot doesn't always mean "holding the line"—your children will and should encourage you to make exceptions, experiment with uncertainty, and even change your mind.

Being on your spot means keeping your thoughts, feelings, and instincts aligned, but it also involves taking your child's perspective into account. Staying mindful of your relationship with your children as life unfolds will help you calibrate your spot to stay attuned and on their side as they grow.

Spotlights

- Check in from head to toe to be sure you're on your spot; if not, wait until you are.

- Use seat belts as a gauge: What are your nonnegotiable issues?

- When you are inconsistent, rigid, or harsh, it's a signal to your kids (and now to you) that you're off your spot.

- When you feel committed and clear and can stay calm and kind, you'll know you're on your spot (and so will your children).

- Since life isn't static, neither is your spot; stay flexible to be responsive to your kids' changing needs.

Relationship, Relationship, Relationship

At the center of every interaction we have with our children is our relationship with them. There are moments when we are poignantly aware of this, but we can also lose track of it in the throes of family dynamics and in the juggling of our lives.

Parenting on a relationship basis means recognizing that the communication and interactions you have with your children shape, and are shaped by, your relationship with them.

When we are mindful of this, the bond with our kids remains strong and central. Our relationship influences our tone and manner, along with the decisions and actions that form our approach—like this:

"Hey, we made a deal that you'd finish your chores before you started playing. First make good on our deal, and then you can play."

At the core of this comment is the parent encouraging his child to do right by an agreement they made. This parent is relating to the child and referencing something that is between them and involves them both (the deal), rather than criticizing the child, which could create contention and distance between them.

This dad is assuming the best—that the kid got sidetracked—and so is nudging her back on track. The tone is one of confidence that the child will respond; they made an agreement, and, although the parent is in charge and setting the parameters, they're in it together.

When you aren't mindful of your relationship in your interactions with your kids, you are actually still shaping your relationship with them—just not necessarily the way you want it to—and the scenario might look like this:

"Hey, what do you think you're doing? You're not supposed to be playing Legos anymore, I told you to clean up! Go do that NOW, and then get to bed. No more playing time tonight!"

At the center of this parent's comment is the message that the child messed up and deserves to be punished, which this parent believes will correct the child's behavior in the future. Here the parent is focused only on the situation at hand, and not the relationship between himself and his child. His tone is harsh and judgmental; the intervention is designed to make a point of the child's misbehavior, to use restrictions in order to get compliance. The parent's message bypasses his relationship with his child, missing the opportunity to build their rapport and to enlist his child's cooperation.

If the parent's message had his heart engaged, it might have sounded like this:

"Wow, great Lego building! I see you worked hard on that one. It's clean-up time, so you can take it apart now or save it on the shelf."

What Vs. How

So many times in family life, the focus is on the *what* and not on the *how*: on what happened rather than how it came to be, how it was expressed, how it affected others, and how you'd like it to be. When we focus on *what*, we emphasize the outcome—the action, performance, and result—and evaluate it with judgments like good or bad, right or wrong, acceptable or not.

When we focus on *how*, we emphasize the process and the relationship, including intentions, effort, and the manner of expressing words or actions. The *how* takes in broader considerations, such as . . .

- recognizing the human-relationship aspects of living together in a family.
- using empathy to consider feelings and needs that aren't visible in the outcome.
- building rapport and trustworthiness by looking at the big picture.

What is the thing that is said or done. *How* carries the meaning and creates an interaction between parent and child. Focusing on *how* expresses to your children that your relationship with them matters most. You demonstrate that caring and connection (the "heart" aspect of being on your spot) inspires responsiveness, cooperation, and responsibility between one another.

True cooperation and appreciation happen on a relationship basis. To make those connections, don't just tell your kids *what* to do, but make some time to let your children know that *how* they relate—manners, cooperation, consideration—affects you and others. That understanding between you and your kids helps keep your relationship central.

Relating to Your Child—or Not

When *what* becomes more important than *how*, parents lose track of true relating. When we communicate, there are three elements to consider: me, you, and the subject of our communication. If you tell kids their room is a mess, you're talking about their room. When you say, "Dinner will be ready in five minutes" or "Tomorrow's game is early in the morning, so no sleepover tonight," you are providing information about a subject—a *what*—but you and your kids are not necessarily relating to one another. In none of these examples do "you and me" become a part of the exchange.

Similarly, when you shout a requirement to your children from several rooms away, you're throwing a message out there but you're not actually connecting with your kids—so you are not relating. In that case, your disembodied voice is not likely to penetrate or move your children the way a face-to-face exchange would. Relating involves connecting and engaging with your children while you communicate with them.

Revisiting the dinnertime and sleepover messages above, they can be stated just as clearly and firmly, but include relating to your child:

Instead of: *"Dinner will be ready in five minutes."*

Try: *"I'm letting you know dinner will be ready in five minutes, so you have time to get ready."*

• • •

Instead of: *"Tomorrow's game is early in the morning, so no sleepover tonight."*

Try: *"I know you really want to have a sleepover, but with your early game tomorrow, tonight just won't work. We'll find another time that will."*

Consider reframing your family culture so that when any of you want to talk with someone, you find that person, make eye contact, and take the time to have a personal exchange rather than commenting on the fly or just sending a broadcast message. While there may be moments in the commotion of daily life where that kind of relational communication isn't possible, or when being succinct is more effective, connecting whenever it *is* possible builds a relational foundation that can carry over to moments when more expediency is necessary. And then, we might turn to shorthand comments.

Shorthand Comments

Shorthand comments, like the constant (and necessary) reminders to your kids to say "please" and "thank you," are ever-present in day-to-day parenting.

Sometimes a brief, firm, to-the-point approach is called for, like when you are prompting your kids to move through routines such as coming to the table or getting out the door, or when a more casual or friendly approach doesn't get your children's attention or inspire the action you need them to take. Short-hand comments include these familiar ones:

- *"Dinner!"* (. . . short for, "It's time to come to the table," when the food is hot and you're calling to people in four different rooms, so one word just works better)

- *"Backpacks and jackets!"* (. . . announcing in a hurry that everyone needs to get their stuff and scramble out the door)

- *"Napkin, please"* or *"fork, please"* (. . . shorthand manner reminders)

- *"Your glass!"* (. . . when a glass is tipping and milk is about to spill, and there's no time to explain further)

Shorthand comments keep things moving, and reminders like these need to be part of helping children learn how to operate in the world. They don't constitute relating, but they provide a reinforcing nudge that you hope will condition your kids to follow routines, use their manners, and attend to social cues.

When kids take the initiative without your nudge to blurt out an enthusiastic "Thank you!" filled with genuine gratitude, it will confirm that your fuller conversations about being considerate and showing appreciation have reached them. It also shows that the relationship aspect of your interactions is taking hold and supporting those times when you need to expedite with shorthand directions.

As that happens, tell your child that it makes you happy to witness her cooperation or to hear her appreciation. Mark the moment to provide a reference point that not only affirms her learning but also lets her know that showing up and expressing gratitude makes people feel good.

When Your Kids Are Too Much—or Not at All—Like You

Just as we can communicate without relating, sometimes our perspective on our kids misses the "relational" aspect of understanding them. Parents can over-identify with children and end up attributing to their children motives, feelings, and responses that are actually their own. When you over-identify, you bypass compassion for your children's feelings and instead ascribe feelings to your child based on how you would feel in that situation.

How do you catch yourself over-identifying? It can be a clue when you find yourself saying things like "We have a soccer game Wednesday" or "We've applied to colleges on both coasts, but we're leaning toward staying closer to home." The plural pronoun *we* merges you with your kid. In those moments, what you call "relating to my child" may actually be sidelining your child and relating to yourself. While you may be tuning into similarities with your child, you can just as easily be missing distinctions.

Challenges can also arise when you under-identify—when you're unable to understand or connect with your child's feelings or experiences—so you can't find compassion for them. For some parents, discovering that their children are indeed distinct from them is unsettling. They find those differences puzzling, and it can leave parents feeling confused, impatient, or alienated.

Whether your kids seem to look, behave, perform, or relate to the world just like you do, or are completely different from you, you're at risk for boundary issues that can interfere with your relationship with them. You can lose perspective so you are not truly seeing your children for themselves. When you parent on a relationship basis, your goal is to do what it takes to get into your children's shoes—but not get stuck in them.

Emma came home from school and told her mom that Sarah was mean to her. Emma's mother was very sympathetic; she commiserated with her daughter and was very comforting to Emma all evening.

However, Emma's mom wasn't quite as understanding a few days later when Emma asked if Sarah could come over to play. "What?? Sarah? After how she treated you? You're not playing with her anymore!"

Emma's mom over-identified to the point of actually holding Emma's grudge for her. Of course, the spat was just one of the ups and downs of a third-grade friendship; Mom was stuck, while Emma and Sarah had moved on.

With the best of intentions, Emma's mom got too caught up in the social drama and lost the perspective that while Emma needed the empathy and support in the moment (although probably not for the entire evening), kids' feelings about difficult situations are often very fluid.

And then—again with the best of intentions—Emma's mom found herself too under-identified to take cues from her daughter when Emma and her friend had moved on from the blip they'd had a few days before.

Had Emma's mom stayed on her spot initially, she would have offered Emma some sympathy and a hug and reminded her that tomorrow's another day. She might have been curious about what would come next between the girls.

When Emma's change of heart surprised her mom (who didn't like anyone being mean to her daughter), Emma's mom could have made her way back to her spot and found some appreciation for Emma's forgiveness and resilience.

When you step away from top-down parenting, you often find some bottom-up learning.

Seeing the Situation from a Kid's Point of View

One way parents can build their relationship with their kids is by looking at situations through their children's eyes. When parents stop, connect, and take time to listen to the child's viewpoint, they're much better able to make decisions and communicate on a relationship basis. Going to your children's vantage point is the starting place for bringing them to yours, and in her family therapy practice, Sheri begins there.

Parents of four-year-old Alex made a family therapy appointment with Sheri; they were frustrated (and exhausted) because they consistently couldn't get him to sleep until 10:30 or 11 o'clock at night, and then struggled to wake him and get him ready for preschool in the mornings.

Sheri started the session by asking Alex why he thought there were problems with bedtime and sleeping. Alex said, "Because my mom and dad make me go to bed when I'm not tired and wake me up when I am!"

Alex looked at Sheri and shrugged—it just didn't make any sense to him, and when Sheri looked it at from his viewpoint, she could see why. Sheri helped Alex and his parents break the issue down in terms of why kids have bedtimes, what Alex needed, and what his parents needed.

Alex asked, "But what if I'm not tired when they say I have to sleep?" Sheri said that bedtime is "bed time." He could lie there and think or wonder, or he could listen to soft music. He just needed to be in bed from then until the morning, when he had to get ready for school.

Alex was content, since this took his concerns (having to fall asleep on demand when he wasn't tired) into account. His parents were content, since this took their concern (a reasonable bedtime) into account also; within a short time, nature took over, and Alex's internal clock adjusted to a schedule that suited everyone in his family.

Relating about these issues turned out much better than the power struggles had because it put the needs of all the people involved—Alex and his parents—into the equation.

Being on Your Children's Side and Letting Them Be on Yours

Parents who communicate their expectations, rules, and routines as part of their relationships with their children, rather than through power, intimidation, or pleading, model the interpersonal skills and social intelligence that empower children in later life.

The key to being on your child's side, even while setting a limit or announcing an unpopular decision, is holding on to the relationship aspect of whatever you're doing with your kids. When you stay on your spot as a parent, you're relating to a child you love, no matter what you are relating about.

Here's a story about an eight-year-old who taught his dad about being on the same side.

William and Anna visited Sheri for some parenting support, along with all three of their kids, to talk about ways they could relate better as a family. One issue they discussed was William's frustration with dinnertime.

William was the main cook in the family, and after a full day at work, he'd come home and make an elaborate and healthy meal, almost always something that everyone enjoyed. Once dinner was ready, he'd call out to the family to come to the table.

Routinely, the children required numerous calls from both William and Anna asking them to hurry to the table while the food was still warm. This had become their de facto dinnertime routine.

Sheri asked why they persisted in rounding up the kids instead of just going ahead and enjoying their meal without them. Quite unexpectedly, this question brought tears to William's eyes, and in a broken voice, he explained that when he was growing up, he lived on a farm and his parents worked from dawn and went to bed at dusk. The only time of real connection between them was when the family was together at the dinner table. That time was precious to him as a boy, and it still was when he became a father.

Eight-year-old Luis's eyes also got watery, but his were tears of anger. "It's not fair!" Luis exclaimed.

"What's not fair?" Sheri asked.

"It's not fair that you never told us that, Dad. I thought I just wasn't listening to you, but I didn't know I was hurting your feelings. It's not fair that I didn't know that!" This began a touching exchange where the kids learned more about their father's childhood and what aspects of being in a family mattered most to him.

Once they understood what dinnertime meant to their dad, Luis and his siblings open-heartedly headed to the table at the first call.

Getting on your children's side, and letting them get on yours, often depends on making your needs and expectations clear in advance, and underscoring your appreciation when they respond. Parents may check in with kids about their needs but forget to be clear about their own. Let your kids know, for example, how important it is to you that their grandparents have a good visit, and ask them to please make a special effort to handle conflict in a better way so that Grandma and Grandpa don't have to listen to squabbles and unpleasantness. And then acknowledge and be grateful when your children get along exceptionally well during that time.

Or, when you ask the kids in the car to stop fighting, they may need you to add that it's unsafe to drive when you're distracted, so everyone in the car needs to align around safety.

When you take the time to share your viewpoint and to listen to theirs, you and your children are able to take each other into consideration and be on the same side.

The Signals Your Relationships Send

Little eyes are watching and little ears are listening to how you manage the relationships in your life. Your young children, as well as your older ones, take in . . .

- the relationship between you and your parenting partner, and what it teaches them about peer relationships, about caring and regard, and about finding a way to be on the same side.

- the relationship between you and your own parents, and the messages they perceive about how parents should be cared for and regarded over the years.

- the role of friendship in parents' lives and what it means to be a host, a guest, and a true friend.

- how you talk about and treat colleagues, neighbors, servers in restaurants, store clerks, and other people you interact with in daily life.

While none of these interactions are between parent and child, they definitely send signals to kids that inform their understandings about relationships—about give and take, about relating directly versus resenting and grumbling, about consideration and inclusion, about how to express caring and appreciation, and much more.

How you build and manage relationships is constantly on display for your children, whether intended or not. This is especially true when it comes to the relationship between you and your co-parent, regardless of whether you are together as a couple. Beyond your relationship with your children, your interactions with other adults conveys your values and also influences your kids in their own relationships, now and throughout their lives.

Spotlights

- Every interaction you have with your children shapes, and is shaped by, your relationship with them.

- Relating positively with your kids sets them up with social skills to empower them throughout their lives.

- Shouting demands from another room may be efficient (and sometimes necessary) but it is not relating.

- Watch out for over- or under-identifying with your kids; stay on your spot and relate to who *they* are as you respond to them.

- Your kids watch how you manage all of your relationships, and that influences how they will manage theirs.

Home Is the Training Ground for How the World Works

What children breathe in at home, they breathe out in the world.

At home, your children follow your every move; they register each response and gauge your actions and priorities. This includes the way you express yourself, the limits you set, the routines you establish (intentionally or by default), and how you resolve conflicts. They absorb all of your behaviors and attitudes by watching, listening, and interacting with you at home. They breathe it all in.

Your children try to make sense of your behavior, even when they notice that something seems inconsistent or unusual. They are profoundly influenced by watching how you resolve conflicts (or not), cooperate, compromise, initiate, tolerate, and forgive (or not).

Home is their social training ground, and they use homelife as a template for how the world is supposed to work. Since what happens at home sets your children's expectations for the way the world works, you prepare them best when you run the household in a way that supports building habits and attitudes that help them function and thrive beyond home.

Who You Are to Your Child

In a child's eyes, parents are the prototype for "others." To them, you represent grown-ups in general since their world is managed by adults who typically have the authority. How you use your influence tells them what they can expect from adults outside of your home.

Family life provides children with their most significant messages about how to interact with others. As a result, kids will often relate to others outside their home as they've been guided or allowed to relate to their parents, siblings, and friends in their home.

The Patterns of Homelife

Your child's outside world is usually organized according to procedures, limits, and protocols. Preparing them to be able to manage within those limits in school, sports, and other social settings is important. Luckily, you have plenty of opportunities to develop family routines and expectations at home that mimic life in the world outside.

Equally as fortunate for you, kids want, need, and typically like the fact that there are patterns in their household. Although you might not realize it from some of the resistance or complaints you hear, the organization or structure you provide helps children feel secure and confident because it's empowering to be able to predict how things will go. Structure also gives kids practice living with boundaries, just as they'll have to do in the world outside.

Actually, most families have patterns in place made up of rules, rituals, and routines that determine how everyone in the household lives and functions together. In the best-case scenarios, these patterns are intentional and necessary:

- **Health and safety:** washing hands, brushing teeth before bedtime, and clicking seat belts before the car moves
- **The needs of developing kids:** evolving their nighttime rituals, figuring out age-appropriate roles in meal prep and clean-up, knocking on a teen's bedroom door before entering
- **Balancing the "want-tos" with the "have-tos":** dinner before dessert, homework before leisure screen time, chores before playtime

These are the sorts of deliberate structures that have been designed and maintained by parents, the ones that you typically feel are working well.

Absent the best-case scenario, "accidental" rules, rituals, and routines take hold as exasperated parents cope with misguided kids.

Daniel was a kindergartener who wasn't inclined to stay seated at the dinner table. He'd get up numerous times during the meal and run around the house, laughing to invite a chase.

His parents usually took the bait; they'd get him back to the table, only to take a couple of bites and start the chase scene all over again.

They'd often end up blaming one another for his disruptive behavior and find that Daniel's older siblings had taken advantage of all the distraction by picking fights with each other or horsing around at the table.

Daniel's family has established a full-blown but completely accidental and involuntary family dinner ritual: First the five-year-old gets up and needs to be reeled in, then parents fight about him, and then the other kids carry on with each other. It's a nightly family dinner show—and everyone in the family can recite how it goes.

At this point, Daniel's parents have a choice to continue with this arrangement or pause and generate a ritual that works better for them, their children, and the climate in their household. To do that they will need to take a couple of steps:

1. Recognize that the existing routine doesn't work well for the family and won't translate well out in the world, and

2. Take charge and reset dinnertime to deliberately form a new approach that takes into account how you would like dinnertime to be. For example, new routines might include reminders each evening that we stay in our seats until we're done eating, having an engaging way to start dinner like taking turns sharing about our days, or offering food that's hands-on and interactive to keep children more engaged.

Like Daniel's parents, you may find yourself needing to become intentional about changing some of your household routines. If your children don't sync with the new approach immediately, they will soon if you are on your spot and stick with it. Kids like and need routines, so they do adjust when the particulars change and stay consistent. But allow for a bit of lag time until the new routine takes hold, recognizing that it's going to take a sustained effort to get there.

Creating Rules, Rituals, and Routines at Home

Young kids typically think their parents are rational and know what they're doing, so they may assume that a chaotic family dinner experience is just the way it's supposed to be. It makes sense then that the children would eventually be prone to duplicating a similar scene at restaurants, in their grandparents' home, and elsewhere if parents don't change the pattern.

While you may become acclimated to your own particular "dinner show," others around you or joining you for dinner aren't likely to appreciate it.

This means that your kids could be met with annoyance and disapproval instead of appreciation and positive interactions in dinner gatherings beyond your own family table. It's embarrassing for you, and confusing for your children, who assumed that homelife reflected the way it would work in the world, too.

In addition to dinnertime, the same goes for staying on your spot and being deliberate about how people in your household talk to one another, treat each other, demonstrate manners, hold family values, and show responsibility. It's tempting to ignore undesirable patterns when you don't personally feel put out or offended. Maybe you don't mind that your school-age kids eat their salad with their hands, ignore adult greetings, or use a sassy tone, but it's important to consider how their behavior will work for them in other settings. Remember to stay on your spot for their sake, even when the issue might not be a personal problem for you.

Because you are the adults who influence your children the most, and because your home is fundamentally their training ground, the messages you give them (on purpose and inadvertently) about how the world works really take hold. Here are five considerations to help you shape homelife in a way that will support your kids' interactions in the world:

1. If your child were to talk to or treat a teacher, grandparent, or store clerk the way he is relating to you at this moment, would it be viewed as respectful? Would this behavior and tone with others reflect your values and be acceptable to you?

2. If your child responded to a friend the way she is responding to her sister right now, would her behavior help her make and keep friends?

3. Does the way your children participate—or not—in collaborative efforts at home (cleaning up, pitching in with mealtime, carrying groceries from the car) make them desirable playmates, classmates, and houseguests in settings outside of home?

4. Do you express your anger and impatience with your child in a manner that you'd want him to expect from others? It helps if you imagine how you would feel watching other adults and children speaking to your child the way you do. The way we show our kids that we're upset tells them how they deserve or don't deserve to be treated. It's an unintended message that can have a powerful impact.

5. Are your exchanges with your children a two-way street? Work to find your spot to create balance so your child is heard and considered, yet also learns to hear and consider others.

Chances are, the parts of homelife that work well and feel good are those areas where you are on your spot and giving clear messages about your priorities and values. Use your head-to-toe inventory to bring that same clarity to areas where you experience repeated frustration with your kids. Become deliberate about promoting interactions, behaviors, patterns, and messages that not only create a positive environment at home but will send your kids into the world with confidence that they can navigate out there as well.

While home serves as our children's base, it needs to do more than hold and cocoon them. Home can be comforting and supportive, and still provide children with the opportunities they need to practice life skills like patience and cooperation. Homelife that is affirming and caring includes some bumps, just like life out in the world; it gives kids the tools to manage and thrive outside the home so that they can be comfortable and confident out there, too.

Spotlights

- What children breathe in at home, they breathe out in the world.

- Kids believe their parents are rational, so their expectations of the world are based on how your household operates.

- Be sure that family life, like the rest of life, includes a balance of "want-tos" and "have-tos."

- Ask yourself if the patterns of communication and behavior in your family will serve your kids in their lives outside your home.

- Recognize that homelife can be a cozy refuge and still provide kids with skills (social and otherwise) for the world beyond your household.

CHAPTER 4

Communicating with Your Kids

The ongoing exchanges with your children color the days and years while you are raising them and set the tone for your lifelong relationship with them.

You want your interactions with your children to convey these messages:

- You are a reliable communicator. They can count on you to say what you mean and mean what you say.

- When you give directions or set limits, it's part of how you love and care about them.

- Along with being thoughtful about *what* you say, you are also thoughtful about *how* you say it.

- It's safe to share with you. You will take them seriously, regard their views, and neither downplay nor overreact to what they tell you.

- You will do whatever it takes to keep the channels open between you, even when that's hard and takes a lot of work.

Most of the communication that parents intentionally have with their kids goes well. When problems arise, it's often because of the confusion that comes from *unintended* messages that are embedded in some of our interactions with our children. While it's not always easy to do, staying thoughtful and deliberate in our communication makes a big difference.

What follows are steps to help you develop a mindset to keep your communication intentional, and to help build a positive communication culture in your family.

Be on Your Spot to Say What You Mean

Being on your spot when you talk to your children means that . . .

- you are clear from head to toe; your thinking, heart, and instincts are in alignment as you talk and listen.

- you are thoughtful about boundaries (who should be included, what your role is, and what your child's role is) and intentions (your purpose in the moment and who is responsible for the outcomes).

- you are deliberate about your message; you choose your words carefully and avoid flooding your children with too much information or confusing them with too little.

- you stay on your spot even if your child pushes back, or pushes your buttons.

- when you need to be firm, you do so without being rigid; you're clear yet able to reexamine where you stand if new information or perspectives emerge (including those from your kids).

Communication with your children is only as effective as the clarity, conviction, and caring behind your words.

Lead with Empathy

When you address your children from a place that starts with empathy, you build important connections that support the message you want to deliver:

- You can relate to what they are experiencing.
- You understand the position they're in, and you can see their point of view.
- You appreciate that it might be hard for them to take in what you're saying and to do whatever you're suggesting or requiring.
- You assume the best and give them the benefit of the doubt.

Children (and adults) are much more able to be receptive, even on difficult topics, when they feel seen and heard. Much of what parents experience as pushback and argument is kids just trying to be understood and to have their experience validated. If you lead with empathy, you're starting off by letting your children know you're on their side, even though they may not be happy with the message you're delivering.

Instead of: *"It's lunchtime—put that away and get to the table* right now!*"*

Try: *"I know you're having a great time and you don't want to stop, but it's time for lunch, so please come now."*

• • •

Instead of: *"No way are you going to that party. You're too sick!"*

Try: *"I know how much you were looking forward to this party and I wish I could let you go, but you have a fever and need to stay home tonight."*

• • •

Instead of: *"Stop complaining about everything and being so grumpy with everyone!"*

Try: *"You seem to be having a rough day; want to talk about it?"* If the answer is yes, stop what you're doing and be there with your child. If the answer is no, then your reply is *"It's fine if you don't want to talk about it, but remember that we love you and are sorry you're upset. Rather than giving us a hard time, let us know what you need so we can help."*

Notice that the examples above are still limited to one or two succinct sentences. Don't confuse empathy with extensive explanations. Also note that being on your spot, being firm, and speaking with accuracy and clarity can be warm and loving. Anything you say can be said with kindness. "Firm" and "kind" actually are compatible!

Manage the Moment

Most troublesome interactions between parents and kids are merely moments in a child's life, all part of the process of figuring out how the world works. Parents sometimes inflame the moment, usually because of their own upset feelings. Their adult-size emotions get triggered, and they turn a child's moment into an event.

Handle each moment as a moment, and don't approach your child's behavior as an expression of a trait or trend until it is. A moment doesn't define your child's character.

Instead of: *"You are rude!"*

Try: *"Please don't use those words* (or that tone, or that gesture) *with me. I don't like it."*

• • •

Instead of: *"You are such a bully to your brother!"*

Try: *"Grabbing that from your brother was unkind. Please give it back to him. Now."*

• • •

Instead of: *"You're a liar. How can I believe you again when you tell me you've done your homework?"*

Try: *"You told me your homework is done and I see it isn't. I need to trust your word, so while you're still learning to be reliable, I'll be double-checking."*

Children will organize their self-image around comments their parents make about them. While you may intend to describe your experience in a given moment, the language you use may end up defining your child. When it happens often enough, that description gets inside them, and children can begin to regard themselves that way.

When you can find and stay on your spot, it's easier to keep perspective so you can describe the situation and what you want from your child. Seeing the moment as a moment gives you a chance to be clear about what matters to you, and gives your child a chance to do better next time.

Watch Out for Inadvertent Messages

Deliberate communication with your children calls for using clear and accurate words, combined with a tone and manner acknowledging that you're talking to the people you love most in the world.

In spite of our best efforts, inadvertent messages are expressed constantly in our daily lives. These examples might be familiar to you:

Inadvertent messaging: Your child comes home from school upset and tells you that her teacher was unfair to her when assigning roles for the school play. You respond, *"I'll have a talk with your teacher about this first thing tomorrow morning."* You mean well, but the message to your child is that you don't have confidence in her ability to manage her disappointment or to speak with her teacher herself to see if they can work something out. Your intentions are to let her know that you're there for her, but you are doing it in a way that relays to her that she's not capable.

Deliberate messaging: You say to your daughter, *"I understand your disappointment. Tell me more about your role."* The telling may help her settle into acceptance or even get excited about it. If not, you can ask, *"Do you want to talk to your teacher about it?"* If she does and needs some help, you can coach her on having that talk. If she doesn't want to talk to her teacher, then accept that and express confidence she will get over the disappointment and make the best of the role she has.

• • •

Inadvertent messaging: Your child is upset that his best friend abandoned him to play with other kids who exclude your son. You plunge into a protective response, criticizing his friend and the other children for their behavior. You probably intend to let your child know that you feel for him and that you're on his side. However, since your response is to mainly talk about the other kids, your child gets the message that what they did matters more to you than how he feels. You may seem to be portraying the world in terms of villains and victims and characterizing him as a victim.

Deliberate messaging: *"I'm so sorry that happened. What did you do and how did that work out for you?"* Later you can add, *"Let's talk about what you need to feel better now and the choices you have if this happens again."* When your child comes to you, seize the moment to truly be there with and for *him*—have a conversation that's between you, so that even in his hurt, he knows you are interested in him and you see him as empowered to be part of the solution. If you focus on the kids who ditched him, he loses you to them, too.

• • •

Inadvertent messaging: Your preschooler looks uncertain as you prepare to hand him off to the teacher on his first day. You mean to reassure him, although—dreading a tantrum—there's apprehension in your voice: *"Don't worry, you'll be OK when I leave today. Really, don't worry, I'll stay right outside the door while you get settled, and then I promise I'll be back to pick you up really soon!"* You wait outside the door and when he begins to cry, you quickly step back in to reassure him some more. Your little one can't tell if your anxious response is about his reluctance to separate or if you are as uneasy about his safety when you're apart as he is. Unfortunately, that confusion is prolonging your child's adjustment to the separation.

Deliberate messaging: *"We're going to put all of our love into one big hug and kiss and then say goodbye. I know you'll have a fun time today."* If you are on your spot that your child is in good hands, your reassurance will be genuine. Then hug, kiss, and leave with confidence. Your confidence will feed his.

Even when you are clear, another way you can send unintended messages is by forgetting to include important information that influences what your kids hear. You might be clear and *upset*, and need to add, "I raised my voice because I got worried, not because I was angry." This additional information clarifies your meaning and attends to your relationship so your child can understand your reactions in difficult moments.

Other times, in a conscientious effort to relate with our children, we include far too much information, inundating kids with details and concerns that aren't theirs to carry, and that obscure the main point we're trying to make.

For example, instead of "I'm sorry I lost my temper this morning," parents flood their children with "I'm sorry I was so upset this morning. It's just that work is really stressful right now. My boss is putting so much pressure on me that I wish I could quit, but we can't really afford that right now and . . ."

When you give too much information like this, rather than calming and reconnecting, the message you intended gets lost. In this case, it becomes about your feelings of overwhelm and pressure; this can add to the effects of your initial emotional outburst by confusing and possibly burdening your child rather than providing reassurance.

Parents communicate inadvertent messages with their actions as well as their words:

- When you agree to stay with your daughter on her bed until she falls asleep because she's afraid of a monster in the room, you may end up affirming that there must be a monster; otherwise, why would you stay there so long to protect her? And you may be unintentionally prompting a routine when she wants you there for protection tomorrow night, too.

- When you constantly hold your older child responsible for interactions with a younger sibling, you give the message that one is always the villain and the other is the victim. Neither of the kids will be served by being cast in these roles.

- When you do your children's homework for them, you're conveying that they can't do the work themselves, or that their own work just isn't good enough.

You can learn to identify inadvertent messages by considering your actions from your children's point of view, and checking in about a misunderstanding when your kids' responses aren't what you expected. Just as you may be puzzled by trying to make sense of your children's behavior, they may be puzzled by trying to make sense of yours.

When-Then instead of If-Then Messages

In their effort to manage their children's behavior, parents enlisting "consequences" often find themselves reflexively resorting to *if-then* messaging. While consequences framed as threats (empty or otherwise) may seem effective in the short term, they often have an unwanted impact on kids and family life. In the most desperate moments, those threats may be regrettably harsh. And milder threats often become pervasive, making their way into daily communications:

- *"If you don't stop screaming, then you can't be at the table with us."*

- *"If you sneak screen time at night, then we're going to take away your laptop."*

- *"If you don't do your chores, then you can't hang out with your friends today."*

Threats sometimes feel instinctive. When faced with pushback, a power-struggle, or just the feeling of being ignored, parents often resort to *if-then* messages to control behavior by threatening a "consequence" or punishment. Often these are loosely, or not at all, related to the behavior.

Rather than feeling the steady guidance and leadership of a parent in charge, a threat signals to kids that parents are off their spot and grasping for leverage. Instead of expressing a clear stance about reasonable expectations, the communication shifts to desperation and power plays.

Unfortunately, this reaction can become habitual, and *if-then* messaging becomes part of the family culture. When this happens, children themselves tend to get accustomed to either responding to threats or dishing them out, which can lead to unfortunate dynamics with siblings, peers, and others.

That said, as most parents suspect, linking outcomes to behavior is an effective way of getting kids' attention to change their behavior. That's because when parents point out where a child's actions will lead, the child reconsiders the relationship between action (or inaction) and results.

You can use that cause-and-effect influence on your children's behavior without threats by simply tweaking your language. A small difference in the words you use reflects a huge difference in attitude and outcomes. While "if-thens" are threatening and discouraging, "when-thens" are empowering:

- *"When you're able to stop screaming, then you can come back to the table."*

- *"When I can count on you to stick with your screen-time limits and bedtime, then you can have the laptop in your room."*

- *"Yes, when your chores are done, then you can go to your friend's house."*

By choosing different words, instead of giving the message to children that you need leverage to keep them on track, you communicate "this is how it works" in a manner that makes sense and conveys your confidence in them.

When you find yourself about to give an ultimatum, it's worth taking a moment to find your spot to make this shift. "When-then" messages are equally attention-getting, offer encouragement and incentive, and are a much kinder way to be effective.

Make Honesty Safe

When your kids share with you about themselves, their friends, what happened at school, or even something they did or said that might have been out of bounds, it's important to meet their disclosures with gratitude for their openness. Always. This is key to parenting on a relationship basis.

Start by telling them you appreciate that they let you know, and then proceed thoughtfully. You want children to feel glad and relieved that they shared with you. Stay on your spot and remain deliberate rather than reactive. This is the moment for your children to share about their feelings and experience; it's not your moment to critique, lecture, or flood them with your concerns.

If it's a disclosure about something that needs to be righted, help them make it right, after you let them know how proud you are that they shared with you openly. If it's a worry, fear, sadness, or shame, give them a place to share rather than loading them up with an overly concerned reaction or "teachable moment" speech. Count your blessings that you have a relationship with your children in which they feel comfortable coming to you.

To maintain trust, always tell the truth to your kids—the age-appropriate, PG version, which means including just the aspects that, at their age, they need to know and can understand. Your honesty will allow them to trust you, which gives them security even in the face of difficulties. Share what you know and what you don't know, and if it's called for, explain what you're doing about it: "We had to take Tiger to the vet because he is very sick. He's staying there so the vet can watch him and try to help him. We don't know if he's going to get better, but we'll find out more tomorrow."

You don't have to *do* anything about most feelings children have. Just be there, and make it safe for them to keep coming back to you.

The Power of "Oh"

One way to be there for your kids is to use one of the most important words in a parent's vocabulary: "Oh."

"Nobody would play with me at school today."

"Oh."

• • •

"My brother is so mean, I wish I didn't have one!"

"Oh?"

• • •

"I got a D on my math test."

"Oh."

After saying "Oh," simply wait and let them talk.

"Oh" may be used with a variety of inflections and tones to suit the situation, but the effect is consistent: to welcome and allow for further communication, without hijacking the conversation your child started by judging or infusing the moment with your own emotional reaction. It lets you just be there for your child as he expresses himself and lets you know what he needs. While an immediate and more loaded response may put your child on guard, "Oh" has the dual benefit of keeping the tone neutral and encouraging more sharing.

Once you have a fuller picture, you will be in a much better position to have a discussion when it's needed and the time is right.

Clarifying Roles, Requests, and Requirements

The more on your spot you are, the clearer your communication will be—and the more your child will want to talk with you. Here are ways that deliberate communications reflect being on your spot:

Be clear about when you're *asking* and when you're *telling*.

- *"Close the door, will you?"* is offering an option, so "no" is actually an acceptable response. *"Please close the door"* is giving an instruction to be followed. Be clear about your intention.

- *"Give me a hug"* suggests that affectionate gestures are required on demand. *"Can I have a hug?"* invites a hug, while leaving your child with the option to decline.

• • •

Be clear when you're in charge, and when your children are. For example:

- A child may be in charge of accepting an invitation (or not) to play with a friend, but parents are in charge of requiring their kids to participate in family activities, meals, or other happenings they might not choose at the time.

- Kids can comment on what meals they prefer and don't enjoy, but parents (the cooks) are in charge of setting the menu.

- Parents set a deadline for when a teen's room needs to be cleaned, and the teenager is in charge of managing the time to get it done by the deadline.

- Parents set a standard for prioritizing homework, and children are in charge of doing the assignments.

• • •

Omit ambiguous phrases.

- *"That's not OK with me"* is unclear and doesn't actually tell your child anything. If you mean no, then say no.

- *"You might want to start cleaning up"* sounds like a throwaway line that could be ignored. If it's really clean-up time, then say, *"It's clean-up time."*

Kids explore boundaries all the time, especially when parents aren't clear about roles, requests, and requirements. You can't blame them for trying! Kids are just following their developmental imperative: trying to clarify who is in charge of what, where the boundaries are, and how the world works.

When you're unclear, it invites children to explore different approaches in order to prevail. It could be by wearing parents down with persistence, saying OK but not following through with action, selective hearing, relentless "yes, *but*" sidesteps, changing the subject ("You never let me do anything! You don't trust me!"), and negotiations.

Some kids develop surprisingly effective debating skills at an early age. Many parents live with budding litigators and need to stay firmly on their spot to avoid inviting major courtroom dramas.

If this is your situation, start by acknowledging your child's position with empathy, and then be clear about your response. If you are already clear about where you stand, then let your child know that. If you aren't yet aligned from head to toe about your position, then have a respectful, informative conversation with your child, and hopefully that can help you find your spot.

While your child may have good points, your goal is to help your young litigator move away from intense, agitated case-building and instead learn about respectful communication.

When you are clear and consistent about roles, requests, and requirements, it empowers children because it makes their world understandable, and it helps them build a sense of responsibility. When they see their parents being clear, they start to make sense of what they can control and what they can't, and they come to understand their role in cause-and-effect relationships.

When you parent from your spot, children learn what it means to be clear by seeing how it works when people mean what they say. And this is how they learn to find their own spot and mean what they say, too.

Communication Dead Ends

Parents most often misstep in communications when they're not on their spot about an issue. If an issue isn't big enough to take on but not small enough to let go, you may resort to behaviors such as these:

- Making comments on the fly while you're doing other things without really connecting

- Yelling to your child from the other room

- Talking to the back of his head instead of having a face-to-face conversation

- Nagging (which happens when you are neither taking it on nor letting it go)

These are dead ends because none of these approaches makes true connections with children. Rather than having an actual exchange, you throw out demands and exasperation, to which children may or may not respond. Most kids (and many adults) opt for "not," which causes misunderstandings and unpleasant interactions that create avoidable stress for everyone.

Your child, meanwhile, is trying to make sense of your behavior, figuring out the patterns that you're establishing, and deciding this must be the way the world works—parents make throwaway comments that can be ignored and then they somehow end up upset.

You shout to your daughter from the kitchen, "Will you please clean your room before dinner?!" Twenty minutes later, you pass her messy room and poke your head in. "Did you hear what I said?" She says, "Yes." "Then what did I say?" "You asked me if I would clean up." "Then why didn't you?" And she replies, "I was going to, but I was busy doing something else!"

The real answer is that you didn't make actual contact with her from several rooms away, nor did you clearly express a requirement; so the off-handedness and ambiguity allowed her to ignore your request. When kids get unclear or mixed messages from adults, they tend to interpret them in their own favor. Take steps to ensure the message they get from you is the one you meant to give.

Communication often falls short when parents haven't first found their spot. Start by getting clear about whether the issue matters to you or not. If it doesn't matter, let it go, and stay out of the "nag zone." Persistent reminders or criticisms confuse children about their parents' intentions and create an unpleasant climate in the household over issues that really don't matter.

If an issue does matter, let your child know by approaching it in these ways:

- Be present physically and on your spot as you connect with your child.
- Be sure your child is attentive to you while you're speaking.
- Say it clearly and kindly, and mean it the first time.

Building on What Works

By and large, we find that all parents communicate well and effectively with their children in some areas, and it's worthwhile to take inventory of the many positive exchanges you have with your children. These are not just the clear requests or requirements, but also sweet moments, fun memories, talking about your children's days, and letting them know about yours. These moments hold meaning, and the connections they form create the bonds between you.

Consider these heartful interactions with your children in proportion to the times you're assigning chores, managing their behavior, or setting boundaries. Work on building up to five interactions that aren't about tasks, limits, or corrections for each interaction that is. This shift to a 5:1 ratio will have a powerful impact on your relationship with your children.

When most of your exchanges connect and add meaning to your relationship with your children, it makes the challenging (but necessary) communications easier—being a taskmaster, setting limits, and asserting expectations. This is also when parents and kids move closer to the feeling that whatever happens, they're on the same side.

Spotlights

- Your daily interactions with your children set the tone for your lifelong relationships with them.

- Remember to lead with empathy, stay with your purpose of the moment, say what you mean, and mean what you say.

- "Firm" and "kind" are compatible and effective together.

- Motivate with *when-then* phrasing instead of *if-then* threats.

- The clearer your communication is, the more your kids will want to talk with you—about everything.

Feelings Are Just Feelings

In the ups and downs of daily life, usually feelings are just feelings, not events. As eventful as your child's feelings may be for you, most feelings children experience are just passing moments for them. Day-to-day upsets come and go.

That said, when you witness your children struggling with a moment of sadness or disappointment, it can trigger your own emotions and adult-sized responses, which may generate oversized reactions that are often beyond what your children actually experienced.

When your own response as a parent compounds your child's response, you can make a little deal into a big deal without meaning to or realizing it. Now, rather than just moving through his own feelings, your child is reacting to yours as well. And you've turned a moment into an event.

It starts with your four-year-old son in the grocery store asking for a sugary cereal that you don't want to buy. You dread his disappointment, so you tiptoe around the issue, giving fuzzy messages and avoid putting the cereal in the cart.

When your son notices the cereal isn't in the cart at checkout, he protests while you try to distract him, and before you know it, your boy flings himself on the floor, wailing and crying. Your dread of your son's disappointment inflated it into a dramatic event.

Or when your daughter is teary because someone in class called her "stupid," and this prompts you to worry about her self-esteem, her social standing, and her academic aptitude. You begin questioning out loud how you're going to contact the other student's parents, why the teacher didn't intervene, and if she's even at the right school. Your concerns are loving, but they are leading you down a path that's far from what your daughter is experiencing. The name-calling understandably hurt her feelings, but without even exploring what it meant to your child, you've upped the ante to make it a defining event.

Remember that it's not the forbidden cereal or the hurtful comment, but *what the child makes of it* that truly matters. Our children's feelings stay right-sized when we're able to stay on our spot and help them address the moment they're having, rather than one laden with our oversized adult emotions.

From our spot, we can express empathy for how they are feeling and, when called for, give a clear message about where things stand:

- *"I know that cereal looks yummy and fun, but it's just not the kind we eat at our house."* You can help your son understand that his cereal choice simply doesn't fit your parameters for healthy food, and this particular nutrition decision is just how it is, nonnegotiable—you're on your spot.

- *"I know how bad it feels when someone says something unkind to you."* Find out what the hurtful comment meant to her by asking, *"What was the most upsetting part?"* That's your starting place. If her focus was on the other child being "mean," she'll need to know how to take care of herself when someone is unkind to her. If she says, "I hate being stupid," then you'll want to understand why she feels that way about herself, and address her needs and her self-esteem. If you can separate your daughter's feelings and concerns from your own reactions, you can know that the reassurance and support you offer addresses what matters to her.

Being There

It's understandable that you might react and slip off your spot when your children get emotional. You ache with their pain, take pleasure in their joy, and worry alongside their anxiety. Yet at other times, their feelings are unexpected and confusing to you and, unable to relate, you become impatient or annoyed.

If you are too closely identified with your children's emotions, your feelings merge with theirs. Similarly, if you are unable to understand their feelings, or your own emotional responses don't align with theirs, it can be hard to connect with them. When either happens, you lose track of your boundaries and your role.

When it comes to supporting your children's feelings, what they need most is for you to simply be there for them. This is where staying on your spot comes in: If you relate to your children's feelings, from head to toe—understand the issue, feel for them, engage your instincts, and ask yourself what, if anything else, is called for—then you are truly there for them.

Beyond that, they need you to understand what's happening *from their viewpoint*, to help put their feelings in perspective so those feelings are well placed and right-sized.

You already know how to do this. When your toddler falls on her bottom and looks at you, it's because she doesn't know if it's a big deal or a little deal. She looks at your reaction to gauge how she should respond. If you have a frightened and upset look on your face, she'll begin to wail. If you are matter-of-fact and reassuring, she'll move past the momentary startle, get up, and continue cruising.

How to Help Your Child (and Yourself) Keep Feelings Right-Sized

The same is true later in childhood. Your children still need you to be there for them to help them figure out how to understand and manage their feelings and responses. The messages we give to our children in their emotional moments help frame what those moments mean to children—whether we're giving warranted comfort or encouragement, overreacting to a disappointment, or downplaying something that is genuinely upsetting. With some perspective, parents can tune in and help their kids find a right-sized feeling.

Rather than make moments into events, kids need their parents to scale their own reactions to keep their children's feelings in proportion.

After James's third day of kindergarten, his mom asked him how school went. "It was OK."

His mom pressed: "You mean nothing special happened?"

"Well, I cried today."

"You CRIED? What happened?!"

"I didn't know where to go after recess."

"You didn't KNOW?! No one told you where you were supposed to GO?!"

Since his mom was clearly off her spot and overreacting, matter-of-fact James got unsettled and then found his role in the drama his mom had begun to spin. He began to cry. "Yeah, no one told me!"

His mom comforted him but was unsuccessful at learning more about what happened. She filled in the gaps with anxious assumptions and was very wound up by the time they got home.

The next day, she confronted his teacher, who was surprised by mom's reaction and explained what had happened.

At the end of recess when the kids usually have PE, it began to rain. James figured they probably weren't going to the playground but was unsure where to go. That worried him and he began to cry.

An older child noticed and brought him to the teacher on yard duty. The teacher confirmed that James was right, that it was too wet for PE, and she walked him back to his class. James's teacher told him how glad she was that there was a friend and a teacher to help him when he was confused about what to do. James nodded and joined the group.

This was indeed a moment and not an event. The moment had passed, although not without fortifying James with the reassurance that people at his school look out for him. It also gave James a chance to exercise his resilience.

James's mom was so caught up in her own reactions that she lost track of him. She missed that he was calm and sturdy when they began the conversation. If she had been on her spot when—in response to her persistent prompts to please, *please* tell her something about this day—he offered up that he had cried, she might have responded with, "Oh," and then asked, "What happened, and how did it get worked out?" That would have aligned with James's matter-of-fact comment while also acknowledging that he had managed to get through an unsettling moment. This was an instance of a parent anticipating, and then creating, a sense that "something must be wrong."

On other occasions, you may *underestimate* the depth of your child's feelings because, as you put your adult-size lens to them, you miss their significance.

Mia came into the kitchen and asked if breakfast could be bagels and cream cheese. Her dad said, "Not this morning, honey. We're having French toast."

Mia began to cry and insist that she wanted a bagel with cream cheese. This surprised her dad, who was accustomed to Mia's easygoing ways at mealtime; he repeated that it was French toast this morning and said that she needed to settle down.

Only Mia didn't settle down, and to her dad's chagrin, she became more adamant and upset. She missed breakfast altogether as Dad sent Mia to her room, and she would begin school weepy and hungry.

Mia's dad was holding the line, setting a firm limit about her behavior, a clear boundary about who was in charge of the breakfast menu. He had clarity and conviction, but he lacked curiosity and concern. When Mia's behavior surprised her dad, he didn't stop to wonder, nor to check in with Mia (who usually loved French toast) about why she was so upset.

Had he checked in with her, or with his own heart and instincts, he might have realized that Mia had been coping recently with a lot of changes that meant real adjustments for her: Her beloved grandfather was terminally ill, so her mom was away tending to him. Home routines were disrupted, and the grown-ups in her family were stressed and preoccupied. The breakfast fuss was Mia's emotional tipping point. She just wanted control over something. That morning she was in need of *something* to be the way she wanted it and had envisioned it.

If Mia's dad paused at her surprising behavior to consider her situation, he might have realized or asked her and learned that she missed her mom. He could have responded, "Aw, I know things have been tough at home with Mom away so often and Grandpa sick. You've been very brave." And once Mia felt seen and settled into her dad's understanding, he might have offered, "I get that you'd like bagels for breakfast, and I'm so sorry but we don't have any here this morning. I'll get some for tomorrow."

Sometimes our kids just need us to lean in, to let them know that we are with them and that not everything is out of their control. Beyond bagels, Mia's dad may want to find other ways to reassure her and provide emotional mooring to hold onto during this difficult period.

Responding to your child's emotional moments is a matter of paying attention to your child's feelings rather than your own triggered reaction. James's mom got overly focused on what she assumed were James's feelings without noticing his matter-of-fact behavior and what he might have needed (or not) in the moment; consequently, she made that moment into an event. Mia's dad only addressed her behavior without being aware of her feelings; as a result, he couldn't get to the bottom of what was happening inside Mia to cause her behavior.

Helping children keep their feelings right-sized means having their perspectives in mind, even as you manage your own—being mindful that if you overreact or downplay, your children get messages from your reactions that you may not intend.

Taking Feelings at Face Value

When parents lose their spot while reacting to their children's feelings, they can confuse the kids and send them off their spots, too. You might do this by overreacting with a child like James, who just had one of those moments that can happen in a day, relating to him as helpless when that was not his actual experience.

Many parents dread witnessing their child's upset so much that they fall over themselves negotiating, accommodating, and overextending. This doesn't give kids the support they need to manage their reactions and to reach out in appropriate ways for help. Instead, it signals to some children that acting out around upset feelings is a great bargaining chip, while it trains others that they might get some relief and diversion by engaging parents in litigating, solicitousness, or drama.

On the other hand, some parents like Mia's dad may also miss the depth of pain or anxiety a child is feeling by focusing on her "attitude" or out-of-bounds behavior without probing the feelings behind it. They might miss that anger is their child's way of managing sadness, or that her bravado is actually masking unease. When children shout "I HATE you!" they really may be wondering, "Do you hate me?"

How do you know when to take your child's expression of feeling at face value and when not to?

You can start by getting a grip on your own emotional triggers, and go back to your spot "inventory" to check in with yourself:

- Use your **head** to get perspective, to register the state your child is in rather than simply yielding to your own assumptions. When your child is upset, scan your mind for recent events or other data points and think about what might be happening for your child outside of this emotional moment. This might help the child make more sense of the upset feelings when you can talk it through later.

- Go to your **heart** and find the empathy to tune in to what your child— at this time, at this age and stage of life—is feeling. Convey that you do want to understand and that you're right here, which will encourage your child to open up and be more responsive.

- Check in with your **gut** and use your instincts to get a sense of what is happening and how deeply your child is affected, while separating your response from theirs. When parents can set their reactions aside and get out of their own way, they can tap into their reliable instincts.

- Use your **feet** to hold you steady unless some response is called for, and then, attuned to your child's needs, go where you're needed.

Feelings and Behaviors

Behaviors your children exhibit and feelings they experience are connected but may be quite different in terms of how you relate to them. Behaviors can be in bounds or out of bounds, predictable or unpredictable, welcome or unwelcome. Feelings just *are*.

While you'd like your children's emotions to be expressed without rudeness, and without kicking and screaming, there needs to be room for them to share their feelings. The key for parents is to understand what's behind the behavior, so they can help their kids express their feelings more effectively.

This can be hard to do. Children often express feelings in ways that confuse grown-ups. Kids who are feeling anxious, sad, or shamed might behave in ways that look aggressive or stubborn. Parents look at the behavior and assume their child is angry or hostile, and then they react to what they see rather than to the feelings that prompted the behavior. If we take the behavior at face value, we can miss what is truly going on for our child.

So when a child who is anxious "misbehaves," a parent is likely to be critical, which can add to the child's anxiety, escalate the behavior, and create a frustrating loop that has nothing to do with the feelings expressed in the first place.

A little girl at a backyard party runs across the damp lawn to tell her mom something, slips, and falls. Looking up through her sobs as her mom and a number of the adults rush to help, she shouts out, "Stay away! I hate you!"

Her mom, embarrassed by her daughter's rudeness in front of all of the other guests, promptly scolds the girl, who begins wailing even more uncontrollably.

This little girl was caught off guard, scared, and embarrassed—and despite what seemed like a rude and angry outburst, what she really needed from her mom in that moment was comfort and help to get away from prying eyes so she could calm down and regain her composure after that very public mishap.

Children need their parents to be able to identify and relate to feelings by separating how the kids feel from how they are behaving. The key is to understand where a behavior is coming from—and the best approach for that is to try to see things through the eyes of your child.

Your child also needs to learn how to see things through the eyes of others. When behavior is out of bounds, if we as parents discern only the underlying feelings, ignoring the yelling, hitting, or rudeness, we set our children up to be continuously misunderstood. Rather than learning to control those impulses, we signal to our kids that these behaviors are the fast lane to getting their needs met. Sadly for them, it isn't likely to play out that way outside of the family.

Children who are hurting and act out their needs with troublesome behavior are more likely to provoke disapproval and reprimands than to invoke compassion and support. This is why it is loving not only to tend to and support your children's feelings but also to help them develop positive ways of expressing those feelings.

The art of parenting is being able to tune in to what to address first. The little girl who fell at the garden party needed some quiet comfort and attention from a parent to be able to calm down after her fall. Once settled, her parent can explain that the other adults were showing concern, not meaning to embarrass her. Since the moment had passed, this information will ideally guide her the next time concerned people extend help to her.

Her parent can also help her learn about how to manage unwanted attention in a kinder way. "I want my mommy!" is a good approach. This sets the stage with your child to say what she *does* want in a positive way, rather than focus on what she doesn't want, which can easily be read as offensive and interfere with her needs getting addressed.

At the same time, when behavior is out of bounds, it often needs attention before you can relate to the emotions that are driving it. A young child who is screaming his demands to come play with him is best supported if you respond to *how* he is expressing his need before addressing what he wants. This is one of those times when the first step is to help our children understand that things go better when they approach us (and most of the world beyond home) in a kind tone and with consideration.

Your child may need your help to contain his behavior, or some space to settle down. Once he's calm and can make his request more graciously, you can respond. And if the moment is right, you might want to find out what had made him so upset before. He might say, "You are always too busy to play with me since the new baby arrived/since you started your new job/since you're always on your phone."

Then you can address, at face value, your child's understandable response to adjusting to change, to missing you, to feeling ignored.

When it comes to figuring out how to help children with their feelings, even when those feelings are expressed through challenging behavior, *remember to be curious rather than furious*. Understanding their behavior calls for you to find out what's driving it. Sometimes what's behind behavior is habit, forgotten manners, or probing to figure out how their world works. Their behavior is asking, "What happens if I . . . ?" Your best response to those behaviors is to tell your children what's in bounds and what's not by letting them know the effects of their behavior.

Other times, behaviors are driven by feelings, needs, and disappointments that don't get addressed by just dealing with the behavior. At those times, stepping back to consider the behavior, relating to it from the perspective of your child's experience, and trying to understand the feelings that prompted it will help you connect with your child and know how to support him. Understanding why children behave the way they do is a prerequisite to helping them feel (and act) better.

While you're attending to behavior in real time, it may be that you, your child, or both of you are too triggered to have a meaningful talk. If so, wait until things have settled down, and find your spot before you talk. These follow-up moments matter tremendously to your relationship and are what help build communication skills, resilience, and the confidence that makes it possible for children to address their needs in a positive way.

Spotlights

- Feelings are feelings, not events—don't confuse little deals with big deals, even when your child does.

- Stay on your spot when your kids are frustrated or upset— that's what it means to be there for them.

- Help your children keep their reactions right-sized.

- Kids' feelings matter even when their behavior is unacceptable, so address feelings and behavior separately.

- Be curious, not furious; children's behavior makes more sense when you know the rest of the story.

Setting Limits

What parents consider "misbehavior" is often kids simply trying to figure out how the world works.

It's our children's job to wonder what happens when they try on different behaviors, and it's our job as parents to give them clear responses and guidance. That's how they learn which behaviors work well and which ones don't.

The Gift of Limit Setting

Setting limits is both a loving act and an essential parenting skill; it requires and reinforces parenting on your spot.

While setting limits keeps family life and your household on track, the main point of setting limits is to help your children know how to navigate their world, including outside of home. It enables kids to understand how to respect and appreciate other people and to function in a social group (for instance, taking turns and respecting boundaries). Setting clear limits also helps children with self-control, and it gives them experience and support to manage instructions, practice waiting, and develop other skills needed to navigate effectively in a world that has limits.

When parents set limits effectively, they empower their children to find their own boundaries and to manage social interactions with grace. In effect, *you're their regulator as they learn to self-regulate.*

Children aren't born civilized. If they were, they'd come to us ready to sleep through the night! Kids have underdeveloped regulators. Year by year, they get better at managing their behavior, but throughout their childhood, they continue to need adults to help them contain impulses and to provide them with the structure and support they can't yet generate themselves.

Limit setting starts with parents setting and maintaining boundaries until their children become capable of self-control. While many parents find setting limits difficult, it is essential for the well-being of your kids. In the same way that our soothing provides our infants with the basis for them to eventually self-soothe, setting limits leads children to eventually be able to self-regulate and manage their own behavior. These are loving acts, and they are among the most important responsibilities we have as parents.

The key to both soothing and limit setting is to provide your children with as much as they need from you for as long as they need it, but not so much and so long that they aren't able to learn to take it on for themselves. Children are social beings in training, trying to learn how the world works. In the moment, your children may not like being redirected, nor welcome the limits you've set, but in the long run you are truly giving them a gift.

What Is Limit Setting?

Your kids need to know what behaviors, language, attitudes, and choices are in bounds and out of bounds. Setting limits is how you help your children navigate the world effectively. When you are on your spot about an instruction and able to engage your children's cooperation, the example you're setting goes beyond the situation in the moment; it supports your children whenever responding to a direction, limit, or boundary is called for in their lives, now and later.

Getting on your spot is key. When your messages about expectations and boundaries are consistent and clear, that is supportive limit setting. If you are inconsistent and unclear, you confuse your children, making it harder for them to understand how to manage when they encounter limits.

The Waffle Chart

The way parents handle limit setting in everyday life helps children understand what's important and what isn't. Here's an example:

Gabriel: My two young children constantly fight over who gets to sit where on the couch when they watch TV. Both my son and daughter take turns initiating. I need help getting them to stop.

Sheri: Do they fight about other things?

Gabriel: Oh, yes. Since our waffle iron makes only one at a time, they used to fight over who got the first waffle. But I fixed that: I created a chart in the kitchen to keep track of who gets the first waffle.

Sheri: Have you considered solving this fight by just hanging a chart on the back of the couch?

Gabriel: Are you serious?

Sheri: Well, actually, charts are for important things, like recording a patient's health status for the doctor, or measuring profits for businesses, or tracking the weather for pilots. By charting who got the first waffle last, you're communicating to your kids that the order of getting their waffle is very important. You're making it a big deal when really it's just a little deal. More importantly, you are telling your kids that "fair" means being equal about every little thing all the time, and the world just doesn't work that way. Rather than teaching them to depend on tracking their turns, let them know you have confidence that they can handle momentary disappointments and manage little deals.

Gabriel: How would I show them that?

Sheri: The show starts when they figure out their seats. Tell them, "When you're settled in your places on the couch, then I'll turn on the TV." Make it a "when-then" instead of an "if-then." You'll see how quickly and cooperatively the issue will be resolved. And lose the waffle chart; it's confusing them about what matters. Tell them, "I'll try to be fair about the waffles, but it won't always work out to be exactly equal. When you can be good sports about either sharing the waffles as they come out or taking turns with whole waffles, then we can have waffles." Meanwhile, you may want to switch to another breakfast item and wait to reintroduce waffles when they are better able to manage how it goes.

Gabriel's motivation in creating the waffle chart was to sidestep having to set a limit about managing disappointment. It's a clever sidestep and a common one; his goal was to create peace by posting a chart rather than setting guidelines for their behavior when they're disappointed. But in doing so, he didn't realize that his children were missing out on the gift of learning how to manage their urges and wants, and accepting their dad's limit about what it takes to be a waffle-ready kid.

The waffle chart is like making deals with kids or relying on rewards for basic things like brushing teeth before bed. Rewards, threats, and bribes may seem like good workarounds when you can't find your spot, but they actually prolong the issue, keeping your children from learning how to manage typical responsibilities without tailored gimmicks.

Setting Limits from Your Spot Is a Loving Act

Since it's a kid's job to figure out how the world works, then it was Gabriel's job as a parent to show his children just that. Sheri helped Gabriel see a more effective way to do this when he shifted from the waffle chart to a strategy that helped the kids understand a basic social premise: When you can manage yourselves and things go well, then the activity (or waffle) will be available to you. If you aren't ready to manage it well, it will be delayed until you are.

Also, it goes better for children when they understand that while parents can't guarantee equality or fairness in every moment, they almost always do their best to be sure things work out in a balanced way in the end. Gabriel really liked the idea of acknowledging that with his kids, and he appreciated knowing that he could be firm and clear without having to be punitive.

Actually, punishments are not truly effective in limit setting. They make the interaction adversarial, engender resentment, and often send the message that "this is happening because you are wrong or bad" and "you have to do time for your crime." Those messages get in the way of the ones that actually help children understand and change their behavior.

Being on your spot lets you set limits effectively and neutrally, without the value judgments, inferences, and recriminations that kids can take personally when parents punish them for behaviors, attitudes, or actions. When you avoid resorting to punitive consequences, you also avoid the sense of shame that reprimands often produce. Effective limit setting is matter of fact: "This is how it works." You put the emphasis on the behavior that needs to be adjusted, rather than calling out your child. Even as limits are conveyed clearly and firmly, effective limit-setting is also kind and caring, and it keeps everyone on the same side.

Children don't automatically know who's in charge, what to do to get what they need, or how to communicate in a civilized and effectual manner. For instance, say your daughter demands that you buy her a cookie during your errand to the bakery. She somehow got the idea that the way the world works is that she barks a command and you comply. She might even have learned that from watching you, discovering that using a harsh voice summons authority. In that moment, your job is to clarify how you'd like her to make requests and to teach her how communication works in your family, and in the world.

This is easier to manage for some parents, largely because some children have more control over their impulses than others. The same is true of adults.

Grown-ups who are even tempered may be able to respond in more measured and calm tones compared with those who are triggered more easily. Kids get the message from their parents about how people are supposed to behave, so if your emotions and impulses tend to be unbridled, don't be surprised if your children's are, too. (A combination of genetic makeup and modeling can make self-control challenging for them.) When parents who struggle with self-control make a special effort to manage their impulses, their children are more inclined to make that effort as well.

When parents stay on their spot and set limits, it helps give kids a container for their feelings and impulses. For children, having boundaries and limits is like swaddling for young infants; it provides comfort and promotes a sense of security as kids develop the capacity to regulate their emotions and urges.

Beyond security and protection, limit setting is nourishing. It is part of a balanced developmental diet for children—think of it as a nutrient, along with care, trust, empathy, and clarity, all of which are part of a healthy relationship with kids.

How Do You Set Limits?

Once you are on your spot about setting a new limit or resetting a routine, keep this short list of limit-setting approaches in mind:

- Making sense of your child's behavior
- Fostering effective rules, rituals, and routines
- Taking it on or letting it go: staying out of the nag zone
- Clarifying "always," "never," and "sometimes"
- Getting past power struggles
- Moving from consequences to results
- Helping children "make it right"

Understanding how each of these approaches works will help you make them your own to set effective limits with your kids.

Making Sense of Your Child's Behavior

The first step in relating to a child's behavior is figuring out where the child is coming from—what's prompting them to act this way? Children's actions make sense when you understand the fuller context behind the behavior.

When a child's behavior doesn't meet the expectations you've set, try to make sense of it. Was it clear to the child that the behavior was out of bounds? Were your instructions or requirements clear? Was the child's behavior deliberate? Was the child in a bind and making an unfortunate decision as a result? Is the child capable of meeting your expectations (is this age-appropriate; are they too tired, hungry, overwhelmed)?

Parents often rush into recriminations and consequences, skipping the essential step of figuring out where our children are coming from and why they're doing what they're doing. Here are a couple of examples to illustrate this point:

The mom of ten-year-old Benjamin was constantly furious at him for ignoring her when she was talking to him. It was a chronic issue, yet until talking to Sheri about it, Mom had never stopped to examine what might be going on. When Sheri asked for specific examples, it was clear that each time, Mom was addressing Benjamin from another room or to his back while he was engaged in another activity (reading, computer, playing with his little brother). It turns out that Benjamin, like many kids, has difficulty multitasking and dividing his attention. Once his mom began approaching Benjamin by making eye contact, asking him to stop his activity for a moment, and then speaking to him, he was nearly always responsive.

● ● ●

At the end-of-the-year school carnival, Camila wouldn't participate in a relay race where a hat was passed among children competing in a run. Camila's dad was upset with his daughter for being unsocial and the only one in her class declining to join in. He took her aside to tell her how disappointed he was without stopping to ask why Camila wouldn't join in the game. When Sheri asked Camila, she explained that one of the other girls in her relay group recently had head lice, and Camila didn't want to catch them from the hat. Camila's dad instantly went from being critical to grateful, and apologized to Camila for jumping to conclusions.

If you take time to get the rest of the story, children's behavior usually makes sense. When you give kids the benefit of the doubt, lead with curiosity, and open up dialogue, you can stay on your child's side as you get to the bottom of the issue—together—to get back on course. At that point, clarify what the child needs from you so that you can find your way back on track. That may mean trying again and doing it differently this time: Clarify whether you are making a request or giving a direction, make your instructions clearer, make eye contact to be sure you're heard, reconsider your timing, or ask more questions.

Fostering Effective Rules, Rituals, and Routines

Children respond to rules, rituals, and routines. They provide predictability, security, and structure that kids can understand and depend upon. Younger kids especially appreciate the feeling of mastery they get from understanding and anticipating family patterns (such as bedtime, mealtime, and holidays). As they approach adolescence, kids are usually more responsive to "policies" (such as "business before pleasure"), which give them some agency in how they manage family patterns.

If you don't intentionally create these patterns, your children will create their own—and these routines may not support the home environment you want for your family. Often, what you might consider unpleasant behaviors are actually routines your kids have established. Once you recognize that, these disruptive and ineffective routines can be replaced by more pleasant and productive ones that your children will just as happily embrace—and that you will appreciate much more.

At bedtime, for example, with young children, parents might want a pattern that goes: first we brush our teeth, then put on our pj's, and then read a story. If parents don't establish that pattern as a ritual or routine, then kids will establish their own rituals and routines based on their impulses and urges. Bedtime becomes "You chase me around the house to get me to brush my teeth, then you carry me screaming to the bathroom, then I throw the toothbrush," and so on. With teens, announcing bedtime may prompt a nightly series of creative tactical delays and evasions. These familiar scenarios can become routines, too!

Because adults tend to have the wisdom to generate routines and rules that work, parents are encouraged to reclaim that role when they notice kid-driven patterns that don't serve their family life. Pause, take some time to make a new plan, and be sure you're on your spot about making it happen. If you're not on your spot about it from head to toe, then wait until you are. That will save you all time in the nag zone (see below). When you are ready, put your new routine in place, knowing that it may take time for it to become a family habit.

Taking It On or Letting It Go: Staying Out of the Nag Zone

Nagging is something that parents do when an issue is in that gray area: It's not a big enough deal to really take on, and it's not small enough to let go. When you can't quite do either, you fall into the nag zone.

- Rather than approaching your kids and really making contact with them, you complain in passing or from across the house.

- You repeat yourself many times, half-insisting you mean it, when actually you aren't fully on your spot.

- You throw out empty threats, even when you (and most likely your kids) know you won't follow through.

The sad fact is, nagging is a parent's way of whining.

So many of our interactions with our kids take place in the nag zone, and yet nagging is a woefully inefficient and ineffective form of communication. It takes tremendous energy and yields little or nothing in return. Here are a few steps to help keep you out of the nag zone.

1. **Mean it the first time you say it.** Parents often save the "final word" for the moment when they've had it and are finally ready to follow through. Save everybody the confusion and drama; wait until you're ready to mean it, and just start there.

2. **Be very clear about whether you are communicating a requirement** (*"Please set the table now."*) **or a request** (*"Will you please come set the table?"*), which is voluntary. Often kids are considered uncooperative because they don't respond affirmatively to a request, when actually they are just choosing an option their parents seem to be offering. If you don't want to be turned down, don't give that option. Be clear about whether you're asking or telling.

3. **Take on one issue at a time** and get it handled, rather than overwhelming yourself and your child with too many requirements or issues to address all at once.

4. **Make a list of your children's behaviors that you'd like to be different.** Choose ongoing issues that you find disruptive or difficult. Then, go through the list and ask yourself about each item: *"Am I absolutely clear, on my spot from head to toe, that I'm ready to address this?"* Circle the items that you are on your spot about—the ones you're ready to fully take on *now.* The remaining items are the ones where you aren't quite clear and ready to walk your talk. Move those items from your "nag zone" to your "not yet zone" and let them go for now.

5. **Realize your limits in limit setting.** You can set a bedtime, but you can't require sleep. You can announce dinnertime, but you can't make a child eat. Nature will help align the child's behaviors with your limits (because she'll eventually get tired and hungry). Meanwhile, stay on your spot until the new behaviors, patterns, and routines take hold.

Ultimately, it's your clarity that most defines how children respond to decisions you make, expectations you set, and messages you convey. You can spare your family a lot of conflict and stress by waiting until you're ready before you approach your children about their behavior. Remember that kids are just trying to figure out how the world works and what's in and out of bounds, so get on their side as you show them. If you are on your spot and truly accept that learning about limits is a gift, you can stand firm in a loving way without losing your message by nagging.

Clarifying "Always," "Never," and "Sometimes"

Your clarity helps your children understand their world in a predictable, reliable way. It helps daily life go well when you communicate with them about when something is an *always* (brushing your teeth before bedtime), versus a *never* (the car doesn't move unless you're buckled in), versus a *sometimes*. *Sometimes* can be challenging for kids.

When a child isn't ready for "sometimes" (sometimes it's your turn, sometimes it isn't; sometimes we go for ice cream after school, sometimes we don't; sometimes you can use my car, sometimes I'll say no), you may have to postpone that activity until they're ready to manage the unpredictability of "sometimes." When you make this clear to kids and they understand it ("When I can say 'not today' without a lot of fuss, then we'll stop for a treat after school once in a while"), those children who are able to handle this parameter often get ready quickly, and "sometimes" goes much more smoothly for everyone involved.

Getting Past Power Struggles

A power struggle with your kids happens when you haven't made limits clear—when you are not on your spot. A power struggle is a back-and-forth negotiation that is generally pretty hopeless for parents, because a four-year-old's capacity for perseverance is typically well beyond yours. Power struggles that exhaust adults can become sport for some kids. You can sidestep a power struggle by getting on your spot so the sparring doesn't happen at all.

Power struggles also result when parents stand firm but do so without grace. For instance, pulling rank with your tone ("I'm the parent, so you need to listen to me!") can invite a standoff. Instead, when you get stuck in a power struggle, move the child along by keeping your tone kind and neutral: "I understand you're upset. We're finished discussing this for now, but if you want to talk about it again tomorrow, we definitely can."

Here's an example of working through the kind of power struggle that's familiar to many parents:

A mother with two daughters, ages seven and nine, raised the issue with Sheri that she needs to get both girls out the door to get the nine-year-old to soccer practice twice a week. Sophia, the seven-year-old, likes to stay put once she gets home from school, so is reluctant each time her mom gives the ten-minute warning that they will be leaving soon for soccer.

When the time comes to leave, Sophia is never ready and invariably says, "You didn't give me a warning." And then Mom says, "Yes I did," and Sophia claims, "No you didn't." When that exchange runs its course, Sophia starts in with another "Why do I have to go?" and her mom explains. Again. Then come the rounds of "Please put your shoes on" and "We're going to be LATE!" Her big sister weighs in on each of these, too.

By the time they get to soccer practice (at least fifteen minutes late, consistently), Mom is frazzled. Sheri helped the girls' mom talk through the issue and find her spot: Arriving at soccer on time is necessary, disruptions to get someone else where they need to be are just part of life, and everyone in the family experiences them on one day or another. Rather than feeling guilty, their mom realized that it actually is helpful for Sophia to learn to accept their schedule and to be more of a team player in the family.

So, once she was clear inside herself, their mom was able simply to say, "We're leaving in five minutes. Stop what you are doing now and get ready." Then, "We're leaving now. We can talk about it in the car, but we're out the door now. Carry your shoes, then; we're going." Mom stayed focused on her purpose of the moment, deferring any protestations or discussion until they were in the car and on their way.

Predictably, Sophia wasn't interested in discussing warning times and why she had to go once they were actually in the car. After a couple of weeks, Mom's version became the new routine—it's just the way that Tuesdays and Thursdays work in their family—and everybody was in a better mood on soccer days.

Moving from "Consequences" to Results

When a child's behavior goes out of bounds, parents generally think in terms of consequences, which is a word parents sometimes use when they really mean "punishment." Instead of devising "consequences" or leveling punishment when your children push a limit, think of helping them understand the *results* of their actions instead. While punishments are ineffective and can engender resentment, results that make sense to your children are effective and empower them—reasonable results help kids understand the impact of their behavior.

Determining a result means figuring out what outcome tends to happen in response to children's behaviors, in terms of how the world works when a limit is pushed. What response will help children learn to navigate this aspect of life and make sense to them?

For example, if your kids didn't stop their screen game in time to get their homework done, then going forward, homework gets done before they play. This is the new pattern until they are ready to be reliable about stopping in time to get homework done. If your teenage driver returns herself and the car home on time, she's welcome to use the car again another time.

Reframing your attitude so that "consequences" means "results" (rather than just a code word for "punishment") requires shifting from the model of punishing your children by making them pay when they overstep a boundary. Results are accepted and most effective when they make sense to your children and you present them as an understandable impact of their behavior.

In sports, this is usually straightforward to them; when you break the rules on the field, then you spend time on the bench so the game can proceed fairly. When you've cooled off, the coach may give you another chance. Recognizing results of behavior is what keeps kids in bounds. When parents understand this, setting limits can become matter of fact at home as well.

Punishment doesn't meaningfully change behaviors and attitudes, but understanding positive and negative outcomes—the way the world works—does.

One way to make the transition from consequences to results is the shift from "if-then" to "when-then" statements (described in the previous chapter). For example, "If you two kids don't stop fighting, I'll have to separate you" becomes "You seem to be having a tough time getting along right now. Let's have you each play alone for a while, and when you're ready to play nicely, then you can play together again." The kids will come to understand that fighting disrupts their play together, while working things out allows it to continue.

You may also be tempted to resort to bribes to manage behavior, and bribes can work in the short term. But when you're on your spot, bribes are not necessary. Using rewards to get your child to go above and beyond usual expectations is fine. But using special leverage, such as threats or bribes, to take care of normal obligations like chores, schoolwork, and manners confuses kids—and it won't help you effectively set limits in the long run.

While punishment can have an adversarial quality, aiming for results instead is neutral and serves to simply realign behaviors and understanding. This takes on a more caring tone and brings parents and children back to being on the same side.

Time-outs are a good example of how a shift in mindset makes a big difference. If you are issuing a time-out to send your child to her room as a punishment to "do time," it comes across to your child as reproach and breeds resentment. If instead a time-out means sending her to her room for a reset, to take a breather and get back on track, then it is usually effective.

The former punitive approach keeps kids in an adversarial role and prompts them to look for ways to avoid "getting caught" or "having to pay," while framing it as a reset teaches them the skill of stepping away to pause, to calm down and collect themselves, so they can reengage on better footing and with kindness. This is a preamble to learning to get on their own spot as well.

What about toys, books, and other distractions in her room, you might ask? Isn't she just going to have fun in there? Again, punishment is not the point. The goal isn't to make her feel bad or shamed or for her to suffer; it's to disrupt whatever behavior had taken her out of bounds and to give her some time for a reset.

Kids strive for agency, and too often that sense of agency is gained by being so disruptive that parents relent to their protestations and pushback. On the other hand, when kids get the straightforward message that they increase their agency and have more influence when their behavior stays in bounds, it makes sense to them to be cooperative.

Shifting away from being punitive and instead relating to sensible, clear, matter-of-fact results is more effective, promotes your children's development, creates a better climate in the family, and cultivates a more mutually respectful relationship with your kids.

Helping Kids "Make It Right"

When your children make mistakes or transgressions, including serious ones, "making it right" is a way of having them recognize and accept the impact (result) of their missteps and move toward repairing them. The capacity to move on from an accidental or deliberate mishap is an important and empowering skill for kids to acquire.

For example, let's say your son loses his temper and knocks down his sister's fort. Once he cools down, you guide him to apologize to her. Don't get stuck on demanding the words "I'm sorry"—any language that conveys caring that he's upset someone and shows a willingness to make it right will do. Let's say your son decides to ask his sister if she'd like help building the structure again. If his sister says yes, then he helps her rebuild, and that makes it right. If his sister says, "No, leave me alone," then he gives his sister what she needs in the moment by leaving her alone. He does whatever it takes to make it right.

Making it right is the goal with older children as well. If your teenager goes out while forgetting to help with the dishes before she leaves, and you're stuck doing her chore, you can help her learn that she can make it right by letting you know she regrets putting you in that position, and offering to take on another household task to ease your load.

The fact is, most parents are already helping kids "make it right" in many automatic ways. For example, when your child says, "Give me another cracker!" and you respond with "What do you say?" and your child replies with "Please," then you say, "Sure, here you go." Most parents don't give a time-out for that lapse of manners; they just encourage the child to make it right with a "redo."

When a teenager misses curfew or goes somewhere off limits, that young person may need to sit out the next round of social activities the following weekend. If you can present this in the spirit of "Take a break, reconnect, reset, and then we'll try again" rather than as doing time being grounded, it lets your teen know that when freedom is taken too far, some trust is lost, and so they will get reined back in for a bit. The family time is a chance to restore your relationship and confidence. This is an understandable result, which is subtly but substantially different from punishment.

Whereas punishment leaves children feeling helpless and angry, helping kids learn to make it right when they've gone out of bounds, made a mistake, or were overcome by their impulses supports them to feel confident and resilient, able to redeem themselves and overcome a difficult time. It's a gift for children to understand that missteps can be addressed, relationships repaired, and conflicts resolved.

You want your children to develop self-reliance, to express themselves and stand up for what they believe. Having clear limits with kids promotes the confidence and competence they need to do that. They will learn from your clear expression and resolve; they are watching you and will internalize what you do and say. As kids grow older, they take over more decisions and manage more for themselves because they're capable of being responsible. When this happens, it's time for you to pull back. As your kids become reliable enough to take things on, you need to let them go.

Meanwhile, until they are old enough to manage well on their own, your children depend on you to set limits. Your leadership gives them what they need most from you until then: a chance to just be a kid.

Spotlights

- What we call "misbehavior" is often kids just trying to figure out how the world works; your role is to help them understand.

- Setting limits is a loving act; "no" is part of a balanced developmental diet.

- Find your spot before you set a limit; your clarity determines how your children respond.

- Children like rules, rituals, and routines, so when you don't establish them, your children will; when their versions don't work, provide deliberate, well-designed ones instead.

- Move from punishments to "results" and "making it right."

Your Place in Your Child's Social World: Siblings and Friends

Y ou help shape your child's social self every day.

Although peers, media, school, and the culture that surrounds them all influence your children from a young age, you still have an enormous impact on their sense of themselves and what it means to be social. Your children are constantly learning from your attitudes and actions, and through family life.

Your children's sense of self is impacted by . . .

- the image you hold of who you want your children to be—and the level of acceptance you have for who they actually are.

- how you respond to the ups and downs that happen between your children and others, especially with their siblings and peers.

- the way you see your children's role in social interactions when things go well or not so well, and what you communicate to them about the role they play in those interactions.

- the confidence you demonstrate (or don't demonstrate) in your children's ability to manage their own relationships with peers.

- your fundamental values and how they are visible when it comes to your kids' relationships with other kids.

The Messages You're Sending

When you're on your spot and deliberate about the values and behaviors you want to support, you are giving your children messages and tools they will bring to their social interactions.

Most of the messages you intentionally give your kids are supportive:

- You let them know you enjoy spending time with them.

- You are caring and show them that you appreciate them, and that they deserve to be appreciated and cared about by others as well.

- You make it clear that you want them to demonstrate and expect kindness, compassion, reciprocity, and resilience in their relationships.

- You explain that many of the social mishaps they have with other kids happen because of misunderstandings.

And yet, sometimes we send unintentional messages. For example:

- Your daughter tells you she's being treated unfairly by another child, and you march off to school to right a wrong you haven't even investigated. While this response comes from a caring place, it may signal to your daughter that you see her as a victim when she reports a disappointment. This directs her attention to the power she believes the other child has rather than the power your daughter can have when you try to understand what happened and help her learn how she can take care of herself in these situations.

- You see your teenage son keeping to himself in social settings, and you pressure him to be more outgoing and adventurous than he is inclined to be. This gives him a message that you disapprove of his way of being rather than letting him know that you notice his preferences and want to understand them in order to support him.

It's important to be thoughtful about messaging in your day-to-day parenting, and to be aware that the culture of your household impacts your kids' social development.

Brandon's family came to see Sheri at the recommendation of his first-grade teacher, who was concerned about the way Brandon was alienating kids when he clearly wanted to make positive connections and have friends. His teacher told Brandon's parents that he was putting off the other kids by behaving like a "know-it-all" and correcting others, gloating about his own accomplishments, and rubbing it in when other kids made mistakes.

Brandon and his older sister lived in a family with parents who were bright, articulate, and competitive, and who cultivated those qualities in their kids. There was much good-natured banter and challenging that went on at the dinner table. Being "in the know" was highly valued in this family, and being uncertain, not knowing, or finishing second usually earned a rolling of the eyes at best, but often put-downs thinly disguised by humor.

The message Brandon got is that being on top garnered admiration and regard, that it established his standing with others, and that not prevailing in a game or discussion made him "less than." Brandon had two gears: pride and humiliation. The shades of social experiences in between—collaboration, give and take, learning from others, uncertainty, missteps, and resilience—didn't register for him at that point in his young life. Brandon was a bright and interesting kid, but he was unpleasant to be around, and interacting with him made other kids feel bad, so they avoided him.

When Sheri saw the whole family together in her office, she could point out the messages embedded in these interactions when they took place and help the parents understand how things might play out when Brandon related the same way with his peers. Brandon's parents were quick to understand how their family culture might not translate well in other settings and recognized that they needed to make adjustments. Sheri asked them to pay special attention at mealtimes when they were all together and to set up an evening each week for board games, which can parallel a number of aspects of interactions that go on at school.

Brandon's parents continued to be achievement oriented, but they came to understand that social skills were also a valuable "achievement." Sheri suggested that the parents think twice about how they were relating with the kids at home, with the second thought focused on how others outside the family might respond. They were pleasantly surprised to find that more consideration and collaboration led to warmer and more enjoyable time together. Since Brandon had been taking cues from his family all along, he easily absorbed the shifts his parents made, and those were soon reflected in more positive connections at school.

It is worth taking the extra step to wonder how your family's ways of relating are likely carrying over into your kids' social world. This gives you the opportunity to be explicit with your children about your values, and about whether or not the way you relate at home lines up with these values. There's no way we can always be our best selves with each other, but we can be clear about which of our words and actions align with our values, and which ones are missteps that we're working to change.

Holding On to Your Spot and Letting Them Find Theirs

Children's social dynamics are especially challenging for parents because more than most aspects of raising kids, their experiences touch on your own memories, longings, and anxieties. As you watch your kids move through the stages of childhood and encounter similar experiences you had, you may be tempted to protect them from the hurtful times in your past and to orchestrate encores for the good times, too.

As hard as it might be for you at times, your children really need you to be on your spot so you are able to keep your boundaries when you relate to them about their social dynamics. They need to be clear about where you leave off (with your memories and pushed buttons), and where they begin, as they navigate their own relationships with siblings and friends.

Your kids need you to know when to guide and support them, and when to step back and let them create and learn from their own relationships. Being on your spot means you bring your perspective and experiences to gauge your children's social development; you also bring curiosity and compassion to relate to their experiences and enlist your instincts to understand their needs. In building social skills, as in other areas, sometimes your role is to provide guidance or action and sometimes—often even harder—it means that you need to do nothing at all.

Don't Underestimate Your Influence

When you observe social behaviors and use them to label your children by referring to them as "bossy," "shy," or "annoying," or when you associate them as "just like me" or "just like your uncle," your kids begin to internalize their social identity with the labels assigned to them in their family.

Saying "That was generous of you, and I appreciate what you did" helps guide your child's social behavior. Labeling him as "a generous boy" defines him in a way that he may be (or feel) compelled to always extend himself—at a time when developmentally, he should be experimenting with a range of social behaviors (including less generous ones) as he learns to engage different aspects of himself in various social circumstances.

Because children feel driven to live up (or down) to your perceived expectations, labels can take children's agency away, and your pronouncement makes who they seem like a "done deal." While you want to encourage some behaviors and discourage others, it's important to give your children feedback and guidance without inadvertently defining them in a way that limits their emerging sense of self.

Your Role in Shaping Your Child's Social Self

While you play a central role in influencing how your children navigate their social world, you don't have a central role in creating their social world for them.

This distinction is often confusing because you are accustomed to being the provider for your children in most other ways. You provide them with meals and clothing, affection and sanctuary, encouragement and coaching, and most of their opportunities to play and learn. Also, you can provide social opportunities by offering guidance and influence to help your children develop values and social skills.

However, you cannot provide your children's actual friendships. Your children need to develop those relationships themselves.

Parents prepare children socially by nurturing their confidence and compassion. You model friendship with your own actions and behaviors, and by welcoming and providing social times for your kids. However, their real social development comes from living through the joy and heartbreak, excitement and disappointment, belonging and rejection, loyalty and fickleness, laughter and tears that comprise childhood friendships and being a sibling.

Your children evolve through these experiences, in the ways they participate and through the feedback they get from peers. As tempting as it may be to engineer their interactions, try instead to devote all your willpower to maintaining your boundaries and staying on your spot so that your children can find theirs. Witnessing your children rejected, saddened, or set back can be really hard on you—and yet in most situations, holding back from intervening and simply guiding them instead, as needed, lets your kids gain the social development they'll need for the rest of their lives.

What You *Can* Do

You can support children's social development by helping them with three important understandings:

- **Boundaries:** Determine what is on your child's side of the line and what is on the other child's side of the line in terms of roles, responsibilities, rights, and taking turns.

- **Perspective:** Discover that there may be another point of view besides their own and that everyone's point of view matters.

- **Balance:** Figure out how they can stay on their spot—find and hold their own place in their interaction with peers—in ways that are considerate of themselves and of other children at the same time.

You can also help your children gain takeaways from the social dynamics they encounter:

- While some aspects of what happens socially are out of your children's control, there are usually ways they can and do influence relationships and responses. You can help them focus on recognizing those ways.

- Being open to the choices, preferences, ideas, and behaviors of others leads to more opportunities to do things together.

- Friendships ebb and flow. In the course of a friendship, there are times when your child will be close with a peer, and times when that friend will be more distant. This is typical and true of friendships throughout our lives.

- Relationships can be resilient, as friends and siblings are able to recover from their disagreements and pick up where they left off. Understanding this will help your children manage those momentary upsets.

- Some relationships seem to run their course and the kids move on to new ones. Change is just the way things are sometimes.

- It can be sweet when a child discovers similarities with others, and equally meaningful to discover and appreciate differences, too.

Here are a couple of illustrations about artfully finding your spot and helping your kids find theirs when it comes to social interaction and relationship building:

It's bedtime, and your daughter is telling you poignantly how she felt left out by a few girls on her soccer team who were excluding her while they were all waiting to play. It breaks your heart to see how hurt her feelings are, even more so because one of the girls is someone she's known since pre-school, and your families have been close. You hug her and let her know that you'll ask that friend's mom to tell her daughter to be more inclusive at the next practice.

Your instincts to step in are understandable, but it's one of those moments when you need to distinguish between your role and hers. It would help her most if you share about the ebb and flow of social dynamics among kids and encourage her to find ways to manage these situations herself. That may involve coaching her about talking to the girls who are excluding her, finding other kids who are more available to join her in the moment, or discovering ways to build more reciprocal relationships with her teammates.

> *Your fourteen-year-old is hanging out with friends who aren't interested in academics and who push the boundaries, such as visiting parks at night where older kids are drinking. You want to tell your teen that you don't like his new friends and encourage him to reconnect with some of his middle school friends who you feel are a better influence on him, but something tells you that might not go over very well.*

As your son is coming into his own as a high schooler, your criticism of his friends and your attempts to engineer his social life will create distance between you at a time when you especially want to keep communication open and maintain your relationship with him. The more independent your kids are in their social lives, the more dependent you are on communication to stay connected to them.

But what to do? You can't control the situation, nor can you let it go, since your son is getting off track. Rather than trying to manage his social life in order to influence his behavior, you need to find your spot as his parent and be clear about academic expectations, about what venues are in and out of bounds for hanging out, and about limit setting (curfews).

And in addition, rather than criticizing his friends, find ways to get to know the kids. Have a place at your house for them to gather and good food around so they'll return. The more of a relationship you have with your children's peers, the more you'll have your finger on the pulse of what's going on. Further, the more accepting and engaged you seem, the more open your adolescent is likely to be with you and the more influence you are bound to have.

Here are some suggestions as you help guide your children through their social terrain:

1. **Focus on the meaning, not the moment.** Remember, it's not what happens to your children socially (that they get excluded, heartbroken, and misunderstood) but *what they make of it* that affects their self-image and later relationships. You cannot control what happens to your children in their social world, but you and other adults can influence what it comes to mean to them. The meaning you help your kids make when they experience setbacks will strengthen or limit their social selves—again, like when toddlers fall and look at you to decide how upset to be—and your reaction directly influences theirs. It works the same through the rest of the stages of childhood, too.

2. **Don't make moments into events.** When children are upset or disappointed about something, they're having a difficult moment. But that's all it is—a moment. We need to let them have their moment, hard as that may be for them and for us; it will pass, as long as parents don't impose their adult-sized emotions on the moment and turn it into an event. And remember—regarding your own children as well as their friends and classmates—that a moment for a child is not a "defining moment." A child who makes up stories is not a liar. A child who is mean is not a bully. These children misrepresent or are mean because they have a need that they don't know how to handle. How adults view these moments and support kids helps keep the moments right-sized—and helps children manage their feelings in more gracious ways.

3. **Stay on your child's level.** Make sure to relate to your children's social issues on their level and not yours. When you bring your adult-level reactions, catastrophic interpretations, parental anxieties, and grown-up spin to an incident between kids, be aware that you don't lose track of where children are developmentally. Most childhood upsets require parents to keep their own emotions in check and just be there for their kids, rather than to do something. At the same time, don't underplay the importance of an experience your children are having by forgetting to keep in perspective what it could mean to your children at their age and in their circumstances.

4. **Ask yourself, "Whose business is it?"** When an issue arises, determine if the issue is yours to address, something for you and your child to address together, something to be worked out between your child and a peer, or something to be worked out between your child and a peer with adult support. Take the time to sort this out and find your spot *before* you step in.

5. **Demonstrate social skills in your relationship with your kids.** You can model interpersonal behaviors in your day-to-day parenting with your children. For example, express your needs in a straightforward way, and accept "no" graciously from your children when you give them an option and you don't like their choice. That will help them learn to do the same. Be honest (with kindness), even when you know that your honesty will cause disappointment; it will model how to stay on your spot compassionately.

6. **Focus on intentions and impacts.** Blame and fault-finding can be diffused when you help kids understand the difference between *intention* and *impact*. What we intend and the way it affects the other person won't always line up. In any given conflict, clarifying one child's intention and then clarifying the impact it had on the other child helps neutralize the drama between them and instead promotes understanding. The focus is on what each child meant, and on realizing the impact, intended or not, they each had on the other.

7. **Making things right.** Finding ways that kids can make things right with one another when there is an incident between them will help them move beyond the problem and strengthen their respective social selves. The child who made the transgression is empowered by the opportunity to repair a misstep, and the gesture offers the other child closure on the incident. Making it right is not just restorative to relationships; it's restorative to the heart and reassuring that even when we have our hard moments, we can get back to the basic goodness between people.

8. **Provide guiding concepts to help kids learn how to manage their own relationships.** Support your children by front-loading broad concepts that they can apply to the dynamics of future peer interactions:

- *"We let guests go first."*

- *"Even if we think something is fun or entertaining, when it hurts someone's feelings, what matters most is that someone is getting hurt."*

- *"When people say mean things to you or about you, their mean words aren't really describing you. They are actually saying something about themselves, that they are unhappy or need to make themselves look tough, get a laugh, or to take their anger out on someone else. I know it's directed at you and it feels bad to hear it, but it tells us about them, not you."*

- *"When things go wrong between you and your friend, think about what it would take to make things better. Sometimes that means taking a break, other times it means changing what you're doing, and sometimes it means you need some help to get back on a good path."*

9. **Aim for apologies that matter.** Kids need to know that we all have moments when we get grumpy or inconsiderate, lose control of our tempers, or do or say things that end up upsetting or hurting another person. Sometimes it happens on purpose, and other times we didn't mean it, but either way someone else got upset or hurt. The best way to apologize is to let the other people know that you realize what happened, you understand how they feel, and you care enough about how they feel to not do it again.

   The next step in a meaningful apology is to figure out if there is a way you can make it right (clean up the mess, make an offering to offset an offense, soothe a hurt). It's not important to push kids to use the phrase "I'm sorry." True recognition and caring are far more meaningful. When you accept that we all make missteps and let your children know that, your kids can bypass the shame that gets in the way of true apologies and repairs.

10. **Welcome feedback about who your child is socially when you aren't there.** Take in the observations of relatives, other parents, and teachers so you have more of a 360-degree view of your child in the world beyond home. Many observations will fit with yours and affirm that you're seeing your child's social strengths and challenges. Some observations may surprise you—that the chatterbox you live with is

shy and quiet on his own, or that your child who seems so easygoing with you really struggles to navigate the give-and-take of peers.

11. **Be mindful that parents are *constant* relationship role models.** Your children are continuously absorbing lessons from you, intended or not, about how people should treat each other, how caring is offered, how upset is expressed, how to get along with others, how conflict is resolved, and how to be straightforward or indirect. Often it's not until we hear versions of our own generosity and forgiveness—or our blaming and complaints—coming from our kids that we recognize the influence we have as relationship role models.

12. **Sibling relationships offer kids a laboratory for social skill-building.** Siblings offer daily practice and continuous relationships to hone social skills and experiment with a variety of social roles with peers. Regardless of their birth order, help your children find opportunities to be leaders, followers, and equals in family life, so they can bring that range of experience into their relationships outside the home.

13. **Provide single children with opportunities for social interactions.** Single or "only" children need continuity of peer relationships, whether with neighborhood kids, close family friends, or cousins they see regularly, to build their social capacities. In particular, they need practice at the give-and-take that ongoing and consistent interactions provide. Parents of single kids can take steps to build reciprocity (sharing, taking turns, leading, and following) into their time with their children: *"First you can come with me to the hardware store and bank, and then we'll do something you'll enjoy."* It can be easy to fall into the habit of contouring to an only child's agenda, which won't help them build social skills.

Helping Kids Find Their Spot

Human relationships are dynamic, and even more so for still-developing young brains. Relationships have their ups and downs and their ins and outs. We want our kids to enjoy the good times with peers and to manage hurt feelings and disappointment with resilience. We want children to understand how to make the best of what is possible in the moment and to understand that most hard moments are just small parts in a bigger picture. Having this kind of confidence in your children won't spare them the momentary heartbreaks, but it will help carry them through hard times as they learn to stay on their spot with siblings and friends.

There are a few key areas where kids often need your help finding their role in social dynamics.

Tattling vs. Reporting

Most children experiment with tattling and need help to understand the difference between *tattling* and *reporting*.

- *Tattling*, on the other hand, is self-serving. The goal is to give the grown-up upsetting information that will get a peer in trouble (or, to make themselves look good by comparison). The adult is being used as a way to get the child being "told on" in trouble.

- *Reporting* is something we ask kids to do for the safety and well-being of themselves, of others, or of property. If your children or someone else is in danger or hurt, or something is being broken or damaged, you want them to alert an adult on the scene. You also want kids to report to you or other adults when they need help of any kind. (This doesn't always mean you'll step in; it may mean that you coach your children about how to manage whatever is going on when that's more appropriate.)

Tattling can often translate into the social strategy of using gossip and disparagement to turn one person against another in order to gain favor. Parents should be on alert to discourage that strategy.

Instead of: responding to tattling by investigating and trying to determine its validity . . .

Try: *"Can you explain, why are you telling me this?"*

Once you get to the heart of the matter, you can help children develop perspective on what their own needs are and how to address them more directly: "Why do you want me to get mad at your sister? Are you upset with her? Let's figure out how you can handle that, on your own or with help."

Villains and Victims

We've all found ourselves conducting a "whodunit" to determine whose fault it is when there's strife between kids. When we do this, we condition our children to believe there are "villains" and "victims" in every troublesome interaction.

The fact is, as we said about labeling previously, putting kids in roles like this (including use of the loaded terms "bully" and "victim") takes a complex behavioral dynamic and makes it static and fixed, which impacts how kids see themselves. Rather than addressing what each child intended and considering the impact of their behaviors, we end up labeling them and defining their propensity or character instead of teaching them how to resolve their conflicts. This encourages them to focus on the actions of their peers rather than on their own roles, needs, and effectiveness, which would help them find their spot in social situations.

If you find yourself caught up in the finger-pointing, making this shift in your attitude toward kids' conflicts will make a tremendous difference. For example, children in a conflict may not agree about the story ("what happened"), but each can report their intentions and how the other child's words or actions impacted them. There is nothing to argue about when intention and impact don't line up; we just need to take responsibility for our own actions and look for ways to make it right.

Grace was running down the hallway, her sister Amy was coming out of her room, and they collided. Amy was hurt and began to cry. Grace kept going to her destination, the kitchen. When Dad went to see what happened, Amy told him that Grace knocked her down. Dad called Grace to join them and, rather than getting into the "whodunit" that generally adds to the problem,

Dad said, "Grace, you knocked your sister down and didn't stop to see if she was OK and to say sorry." Grace replied indignantly, "But it wasn't my fault. She walked into me!"

Dad explained that he understood that she hadn't intended to hurt her sister. However, when they collided, her sister did get hurt, and Grace's body had a role in that, so she has some responsibility for the impact. She can address the impact she had by showing her sister that she has concern and feels bad that her sister was hurt, and also let Amy know that Grace didn't intend to hurt her. He told Amy that it's important to be gracious and to be able to forgive when someone is genuinely concerned and sorry about hurting her. He gave the example of being jostled on a bus ride and bumping into another passenger. Even though it wasn't his fault, he still took responsibility, and let the other person know he was sorry. Dad told both girls that he'd like his kids to extend that same courtesy and care to one another and to others as well.

Their father found a way to address the interaction without casting either of the girls in the roles of villain or victim. Instead, he helped them understand the importance of the intentions behind their actions and the impacts their actions have. His modeling will help the girls carry this approach into other situations as well.

If you see the victim/villain pattern repeating in a setting outside the home, reach out to an adult on the scene—perhaps a teacher or another parent. Since you can't always be there, it's important to figure out how you can work together to support your child and the other children to break from the cycle of blame and helplessness. If this is something that happens continuously in your family or with your child in various settings, reach out to a counselor or parenting coach for help to get your child on a better track socially.

Inclusion and Exclusion

In the spirit of keeping feelings right-sized, remember that kids' friendships and their standing with siblings are often fluid, so social ins and outs are to be expected. When children feel left out, it is often painful for them and sad for you. There's a temptation to intervene and force a solution. However, like friendships, inclusion cannot be legislated by parents; it needs to be inspired by the children themselves. You can support your children's ability to manage themselves so that others will want to include them, and you can encourage generosity so that they will be inclined to include others.

Your kids will inevitably exclude and be excluded, but the actual instance of exclusion is much less important than the way your children handle it. When children learn to exclude with kindness and compassion ("I want to just read on my own right now, but maybe we can hang out after dinner"), being turned down is just one of the outcomes among many that a child experiences in the course of a day. When your child excludes unkindly ("Get out of here; I don't want you in my room!"), it can become a hurtful incident.

Aim to support your children to be gracious and kind when disappointing peers, and to encourage their siblings and friends to express themselves kindly, too. You can also strive to support your "excluded" child to accept "no" with grace and respect, and to help others do the same. Offer language to help your child exclude with kindness, and to move through being excluded:

- *"Sam and I want to just play alone together right now, but maybe we can play with you later."*
- *"Oh well, if it can't work out this time, I hope we can play another time."*

Their experiences with navigating inclusion and exclusion can provide kids with opportunities to build values, social skills, and confidence.

A third-grade child in Sheri's practice, Julia, had been close friends with Alyssa since kindergarten. Then in third grade, Alyssa became friends with a new girl, Victoria. Victoria wanted an exclusive relationship with Alyssa, and she put a lot of pressure on Alyssa to "break up" with Julia, encouraging Alyssa to tell Julia that she no longer wanted to be friends. Alyssa did just that, which devastated Julia and, in turn, devastated Julia's mom.

Julia's mom and Julia checked in with Sheri. After clarifying how Julia felt, Sheri helped Julia understand that what Alyssa said told her something about Alyssa and Victoria, but it didn't reflect on Julia or her feelings. She suggested that Julia find her own spot and be clear with Alyssa about where she stood. She advised Julia that while it might not change the situation, at least she can let her friend know how she feels. Sheri asked Julia to think about what she wanted Alyssa to know and to find a time to say that to her.

Julia gave it serious and careful thought. She approached Alyssa the next day at school and said, "Even if you don't want me to be your friend, I want you to know that I still really like you and you will always be my *friend." Julia had no expectations, so she was surprised when Alyssa began to cry, apologized for being "mean," and said that Julia will always be her friend, too. Further, Alyssa made this clear to Victoria, and while Alyssa split her time initially, the three girls eventually ended up all becoming friends.*

"Popularity"

Parents often measure their children's social development by their level of popularity: how many playdates and birthday parties they are invited to, how many kids are in the crowd they hang out with, how much online attention they attract, and so on.

When you're wondering how your child is doing socially, it's important to recognize that "popularity" and "friendship" are not the same thing. In the long run, popularity doesn't really matter, but true friendship does.

For example, popularity doesn't predict future happiness or well-being, while having at least two or three good friends does. The skills kids employ to be popular might help them run for public office or succeed in a marketing career, but they are not the skills it takes to build genuine, lasting friendships. Parents with their eye on their child's popularity are not paying attention to the social skills that matter—and that will equip kids for a lifetime of caring and meaningful relationships with friends, partners, family, and colleagues.

Those skills include empathy, compassion, collaboration, loyalty, forgiveness, and resilience.

As Your Kids Move into and through Adolescence

When your children begin to take their own paths socially and start planning independent activities with peers, it becomes even more challenging to find your place. This is supposed to happen; it's a kid's job to gradually demote their parents.

Still, even in their budding independence, your kids need you to be attuned to their social world, to know their friends, to set guidelines about comings and goings and in-bounds and out-of-bounds activities. And as they demonstrate their maturity and capacity as social beings, their choices of friends, their interests, and their notions of privacy become increasingly their own.

The most important role you have as the parent of a teenager, as your kids push the boundaries for autonomy, is to encourage the kind of open communication and sharing that maintains your access to their inner and outer selves. You will always be influential to your children, no matter what, but the more you stay on your spot and use your best communication skills, the better you will know and understand what is happening in their lives and the more deliberate, helpful, and well directed your influence can be. All of this groundwork, patience, and caring will likely support your relationship with your children even after they've left home.

Remembering Your Spot and Theirs

Given your own childhood memories, along with any sensitivities or aspirations you may carry about your own social self, it takes concentrated effort to hold on to your spot around kids' relationships with siblings and peers. Because our personal experiences and roles in the mix can be confusing, we tend to lose our footing and under- or over-involve ourselves.

A simple way of knowing when to step in is to ask yourself if your child . . .

- lacks the experience to recognize the impact of their behavior or the behavior of the other child(ren).

- is on the giving or receiving end of out-of-bounds behavior.

- is at risk for being physically or emotionally hurt beyond the typical ups and downs of kids' social lives.

- uses language or behavior that's out of alignment with your family's values.

- lacks the language or behavioral tools to manage the interaction or circumstances without your help.

In any of those circumstances, your role is to understand your children's experience and to provide them with this support to help them cope:

- **perspective** about human nature and ways of being, and about the impact of actions

- **information** about what's appropriate, acceptable, and allowed according to your values (regarding how they should treat and be treated by others, what is in and out of bounds with the language and behavior they use or experience)

- **tools** that help them express their needs and set limits, determine when to persist and when to let go, and learn how to step back and ask for help

Supporting your children's social development involves letting them find their own way through fun, excitement, disappointments, joy, and tears—all of which are the building blocks of friendship and the skills needed to relate to others. If you stay on your spot, you will be able to give your kids room so they can learn for themselves, and you'll be there for them when they need to learn from you.

Spotlights

- Stay on your spot as you consider when to step in and when to step back to let your kids develop their own relationships.

- Recognize the impact your messages are having on your children's self-image and social development.

- Rather than relating to kids as villains or victims, focus on your child's role in the dynamics.

- Help your children understand the difference between intention and impact, and to consider both.

- Know that while you can't control what happens to your kids socially, you can influence what their interactions mean to them.

Supporting True Self-Esteem

Children need to know two things to feel good about themselves: that they're unique and special *and* that they're just like everybody else.

The art of parenting is knowing when to give which message.

True self-esteem is based on our capacity to regard ourselves and others at the same time. It means that caring and consideration are both inward and outward facing. So, to experience a genuine and full sense of self-esteem, children need to develop an understanding of themselves as distinct and special, and at the same time, realize they have a lot in common with the rest of humanity.

Letting Your Kids Know They Are Unique and Special . . .

You want to help your children recognize what is unique about them and let them know that they matter as individuals. While that recognition for kids may begin as a response to feedback from others, it needs to take hold within them, intrinsically. Often parents mistakenly view their children's self-esteem as dependent on continuous recognition for their performance.

Encouraging and praising your children's skills, deeds, and accomplishments helps promote their self-regard. But doing it constantly also trains them to perpetually look outward for approval and affirmation from others to build their sense of confidence and worth, and this actually *undermines* their self-esteem.

Children who are accustomed to their parents making a big to-do about everything they do will naturally expect the same from peers and other adults. These kids end up feeling disappointed when others don't shine the same spotlight on them—which inevitably will happen in the demanding and often indifferent world outside of home.

Children who constantly need to be first, or fastest, to hog the ball or always know the right answer, fall into this pattern. They are incessantly looking outward for praise, using competition and comparison as measures of their worth. Rather than self-esteem, these children are actually revealing their insecurity.

You already know how to show your children that they are special and truly matter. Remember how much you adored your newborn when you first looked into her eyes, or the affection you felt when she dropped and then picked up her sippy cup? Do you recall your concern when she told you she was scared, or your delight at her first drawing, or the time you changed your mind because she made a good point?

Think about the time you devote to her now—supporting her activities, listening, talking, and sharing experiences. These are the things you do because you genuinely like her and love her and get a kick out of who she is.

Now, find those feelings inside and focus on your child's unique ways of being rather than her growing résumé, and you'll have everything you need to help your child know that she is special.

Instead of piling on the compliments and tributes for outcomes and accomplishments, let your kids know what you observe and appreciate about *how* they approach things. If what you comment about is truly observable, it will be seen and commented on by others as well and will help your children understand the qualities they bring, and how those strengths are regarded by others.

Matthew's parents were caring for their two young nieces, ages seven and nine, for the weekend. The older of those girls, Talia, was very outgoing and had an easy time connecting with others. The other, Anya, was very quiet and seemingly withdrawn. Matthew's parents were determined to show the girls a good time but felt concerned that Anya seemed disengaged and unhappy.

Matthew, age twelve, was doing his best to be a good host. Noting his parents' worry, he kept an eye on Anya. At one point Matthew overheard Anya say to Talia, in the softest voice, "I'm having such a good time!" Matthew went to his parents and shared what he heard and added, "I think maybe when Anya is happy, she doesn't show it. We should just ask her how she's feeling."

Instead of telling Matthew how brilliant and sensitive he is, Matthew's mom said, "I really appreciate how you paid attention to Anya so that you were able to hear her comment and realize that we were misunderstanding her. It's great that you can notice things about people that help you understand them better."

Rather than defining and characterizing Matthew, his mom was able to describe what he did and to make him aware of a capacity he has and how he used it well. When we can point out abilities that we observe in our kids, they learn to recognize these attributes in themselves and bank on them. It helps them build their personal "tool kit" and, along with that, a reliable self-image.

Knowing we matter comes from being seen and heard, and from realizing we have an effect on and can influence others. This awareness helps children *be* in the world, as a part of a team, class, or community, with a positive sense of self.

. . . and Just Like Everybody Else!

A child's self-regard is only half of the self-esteem equation. To have true self-esteem, kids also need to know they're just like everyone else. Everyone else has feelings, needs, and desires, too. Everyone else has ideas, wants to have a turn, yearns to be seen and appreciated. Everyone else has moments when they get stuck, are confused, and make mistakes. We all have strengths and talents, insecurities and challenges, and we all matter.

When children are doing or feeling something that they like, it's affirming to know that there are other people who do and feel the same way. And when kids experience something that they don't like, it's comforting for them to understand that others go through these difficulties, too. It is a gift when you can help children realize that they aren't alone in the world.

Celebrating common milestones (birthdays and graduations, for example) helps unite us with others who share the experience or achievement. The same is true of celebrating other smaller but still significant passages—losing a first tooth, learning to ride a bicycle, getting a driver's license, and so on. We celebrate when we join the ranks of others who have also attained or experienced what we have, and we like the sense of belonging that it brings.

If you help your kids understand that we are all more similar than different, then they will develop the capacity to recognize how other people feel and respond, how to get in their shoes (empathy), and what makes humans tick. Further, you're helping them become more comfortable expressing how things are for them—because they will know that while people may not always agree with each other, everyone else has ideas, feelings, and needs just like they do.

Having this kind of connection to others—while holding on to their sense of their uniqueness and individual worth—allows kids to feel a part of (instead of needing to be set apart from) the people in their world. Genuine self-esteem is a two-way street that connects us to others and them to us.

Sean's family was working with Sheri when Sean brought up that he was feeling sorry for himself because reading was so hard for him, and seemed so much easier for other kids. He hated feeling different. His parents were sympathetic and tried to ease things for Sean. What they hadn't mentioned to him, though, is that while this is really tough for Sean, everybody struggles with something that others seem to do more easily, whether it shows or not. When Sheri told Sean that, he said, "Yeah, but nothing is as bad as when reading is your hard thing." Sheri replied, "That's what everybody says about their hard thing!

Whatever hard thing is yours is the one that feels the hardest." Sean laughed. It made him feel better to know he was more alike than different from other kids.

Elena's mom asked her to help carry groceries into the house and to set the table for dinner. Elena grumbled a bit but rather than putting up her usual level of resistance, she just did the tasks and then asked if she could have extra time on the computer because she had been so helpful. Her mom almost said yes, because she was indeed grateful for Elena's cooperation, but then realized that the message to Elena would be that helping out around the house when asked is exceptional. Instead, she said to Elena, "I really appreciate your help, but it doesn't mean extra screen time. Helping each other is just what we do in this family." That let Elena know her contributions to the family mattered, just like everyone's contributions do.

Some Markers of True Self-Esteem

Kids whose self-regard is both inward and outward facing are more likely to view differences with wonder and interest rather than fear and distrust. It also helps them view others as peers rather than rivals. This ability helps kids feel more centered and connected and reflects true self-esteem.

One marker of true self-esteem is humility, knowing ourselves as we truly are. Humility is sometimes mistaken for low self-esteem. But actually, people with humility recognize their inner value and also accept their limitations and how they fit in relation to others. Humility allows kids to appreciate the abilities or accomplishments of others, accept their own challenges, and be willing to take risks and be vulnerable because they aren't deterred by making mistakes.

Other markers of true self-esteem show up in children who . . .

- are able to say what they want and are also mindful of their impact on others (*"Excuse me for interrupting, but I have a question."*).

- enjoy their own success and also show appreciation for the success of others, such as complimenting a sibling or friend and being genuinely glad when that child is recognized.

- not only do their best but also bring out the best in others.

- are comfortable enough about their sense of self and relation to others that they embrace people with curiosity, compassion, and generosity.

- ask for help when they need it, acknowledge mistakes when they make them, and receive instruction or corrections without getting defensive. They feel sturdy enough to know that needing help, making mistakes, and hearing corrections are just that—rather than a comment on their self-worth. (Kids who instead have quick "shame triggers" usually don't feel worthy, and don't believe that they are "just like everybody else." Instead, they feel or fear that they are less-than.)

Building True Self-Esteem from Your Spot—and Theirs

True self-esteem is key to being able to find and stay on your spot. Finding your spot starts with knowing that your spot matters. It means being able to connect with what you think, feel, intuit, and are prepared to do. To find your spot, you need to have a sense of yourself and an awareness of others; you have to be able to hold both at the same time.

To stay on your spot and guide your kids to find their own in building their self-esteem, you can model and help them embrace these empowering perspectives:

- **Make the best of circumstances instead of needing them to be the best.** Children who can make the best of what they have, rather than needing the "best" or getting exactly what they want, learn to make meaning from their experiences rather than letting their experiences define their well-being. We can't control what does and doesn't come our way or how things turn out, but how we deal with what life presents us is a reflection of how we feel about ourselves.

    For example, helping your children embrace an "Oh well" response helps a disappointment pass so they can move on to accepting what is, rather than being stuck in personalizing the upsetting moment.

- **Express gratitude and appreciation.** Your children's gratitude and appreciation demonstrate their having recognized, accepted, and internalized the caring, thoughtfulness, and generosity of others. Their gratitude shows that they appreciate their relationships, and that reflects the value they place on the people in their world. Encourage your children to be receptive to the thoughtful and caring gestures of people around them and to acknowledge those who have reached out to connect with them.

    Parents may see a lack of gratitude or appreciation as an indicator of entitlement or selfishness, when actually, it often illustrates that the child isn't really taking in the caring gestures of others—a possible indicator of low self-esteem. Kids who don't take in what is being given to them miss the opportunity to feel regarded and to know they matter.

- **Accept boundaries and responsibilities.** Children who understand what's theirs to manage and what others are responsible for are more able to ask for and be grateful for help when they need it—and to offer help when others need it. This understanding is central for kids to feel like they fit into a family, group, or community. That sense of belonging is another key to true self-esteem. Knowing what *isn't* yours to manage makes it possible to identify what *is* yours, which helps you find and stay on your spot.

How True Self-Esteem Plays Out

Children with self-esteem stand out. They're the team players, the kids who take joy in seeing others excel, who are excited by participating in collaborative efforts.

Consider the budding actor who fills the stage in a bit part, or the soccer player who prides herself on making assists as much as scoring goals, or the high school senior who celebrates his admission to the colleges he *did* get into and is excited for his friends about their acceptances, or the young woman who speaks her mind to her parents in a way that is considerate and respectful.

These are kids who feel good about themselves, who relate to and appreciate others, who adults recognize, and who their peers want to be around. This is what happens when self-esteem is a two-way street.

Spotlights

- To have true self-esteem, kids need to know two things: that they're unique and special—and they're just like everyone else.

- When children have true self-esteem, their interactions include both self-regard and regard for others.

- Avoid excessive praise, which directs kids to look outward for affirmation rather than recognizing their own worth.

- Humility is sometimes mistaken for low self-esteem, but actually, people with humility understand that their limitations mean they are human . . . just like everybody else.

- Your children's expressions of gratitude show they have taken in the caring and generosity of others, which allows them to feel regarded and know they matter.

CHAPTER 9

Exercising the Disappointment Muscle and Other Ways to Build Resilience

Parents long to give their children the gift of protection from all hurts and upsets. Sadly, this gift is not ours to give. What we can give them is our help to develop their resilience—which may be the most important gift of all.

We can't control what difficulties our children will have to face, but the ability to endure and make the best of routine disappointments is key to their well-being. By helping our children learn to manage and bounce back from everyday letdowns, we help them gain the capacity and confidence to deal with the bigger setbacks and losses that life can bring.

What Does Resilience Look Like in Everyday Family Life?

Resilience is having faith that . . .

- things will work out, and you can usually find a way to do something about the difficulties you face.

- when you can't do something to improve a situation, you know that you can handle your feelings, and that the intensity of your sadness and upset will eventually subside.

- even in the midst of a hard time, you can find and appreciate the good around you.

- rather than needing circumstances to be the best, you can make the best of circumstances.

Unfortunately, it is not uncommon for kids to have a difficult time dealing with disappointment. Some have real struggles when it's time to turn off the screen, when they don't make a sports team or get the grade they hoped for, when a cherished friend prefers to be with someone else, or even when dinner isn't something they like. These young people—from toddlers to college students—need some help to learn to handle everyday disappointments.

Maya's teacher reported to her parents that she was having a tough time in fourth grade. The teacher said that Maya seemed to have overly sensitive responses to small incidents throughout her day. For instance, if the teacher complimented another student's efforts, Maya would sulk because her own work hadn't been singled out. When Maya's friend chose another girl to play with at recess, Maya burst into tears, needing a lot of comfort from the yard duty teacher that lasted well beyond the end of recess. The teacher shared that when things didn't go Maya's way, even small, transient issues, her reactions were overly emotional. As a result, Maya's peers had begun to avoid her.

When Sheri met with Maya and her family, she asked Maya if things were as hard for her at home as they were at school. Maya said no, and that she was always happy at home. Sheri began a series of "what if" questions, and quickly got the picture.

"What if you don't like what is served at dinner?"

Maya replied, "My mom makes me something else I do like, like macaroni and cheese."

"What if your brother won't play the game you want to play?"

Her brother piped up, "My parents make me play what she says so she won't scream and cry and ruin everybody's time."

"What if you're not ready to go to bed when it's bedtime?"

Maya answered, "My dad stays with me and talks to me until I fall asleep."

The situation was clear: Maya was not being allowed to have the experiences that would exercise her "disappointment muscle," or the chance to let her upset feelings run their course so she could have confidence in being able to move past them. Maya's parents treated her as if she were too fragile to manage everyday upsets.

In an effort to keep Maya (and themselves) comfortable, Maya's parents had been contouring family life to all of Maya's wants, and this left her without the opportunity to develop internal resources to manage the inevitable situations outside the home where her parents couldn't provide that service. Consequently, Maya was developmentally behind the other kids her age in being able to handle the ups, downs, ins, and outs of a nine-year-old's world.

Constantly arranging and managing family life, school, and commitments to adjust to your children's comforts and wants doesn't allow them to learn to navigate when things don't go their way. You may believe it's easier or kinder to constantly give in, but this actually holds kids back. When children get chances to face and move past disappointment, they feel more capable of taking on challenges that don't have a guaranteed outcome. This is an extraordinary gift we all want to—and can—give our children.

What Is the "Disappointment Muscle," and How Does It Work?

Think of it this way: Kids are born with a disappointment muscle that needs to be exercised so they develop the strength to handle setbacks and discouragements. This is challenging for a lot of parents whose instinct is to help their children *avoid* disappointment. You cross the street rather than pass a bakery so you don't have to say "no" to your children's requests for cookies. You reshuffle the cards when your kids aren't looking to stage their "victory" in the game. You say, "We'll see" when you mean "No," and then find all sorts of creative work-arounds to sidestep your kids' displeasure.

Sometimes when we maneuver to spare our children from disappointment, it's because we dread the sulking, defiance, and tantrums that tend to follow when they don't get what they want. Even when we find our spot, we may convey an anticipatory flinch at the very thought of those difficult behaviors for which we're bracing ourselves. Our kids see the flinch on our face and mistake it for evidence that even *we* think saying "no" is terrible!

Staying on your spot means being sure-footed when your children express upset or discontent. When the sulking or tantrums happen, you continue to convey that while you understand they're disappointed, this is just how this moment is going to go, so they may as well make the best of it. (And you may have to make the best of the period of sulking and tantrums until your children realize those behaviors don't influence you anymore.)

The more experience kids have with managing disappointment, the stronger their disappointment muscles will grow and the easier the next disappointment will be for them—and for you.

The good news is that helping your children build their disappointment muscle is one of the most convenient aspects of everyday parenting. It doesn't require arranging a carpool, paying for a special class, or hiring a coach or tutor. Life offers plenty of opportunities for children to be disappointed, sometimes repeatedly, at home and in the world, all free of charge!

Your kids may want you to keep interacting with them when it's time for lights out, or to negotiate going to a sleepover when you've said no, or to extend their curfew, or to waive their chores, or to give them another cookie. They may really want to play the video game you vetoed. The list goes on and on—disappointment awaits every child. All parents need to do is let them learn to manage their upset.

As counterintuitive as it may seem, when things don't go their way, it's healthy to allow our children opportunities to feel sad, left out, and let down, to offer our compassion and then help them move on to whatever is next. Friendships begin and end, games are lost, toys are misplaced, hearts are broken, and from time to time, a big curveball throws them off. It all goes so much better when children have some inner strength to flex when disappointment inevitably comes their way. The process of learning how to handle letdowns is essential to becoming a resilient, confident, and happy person, and the job of teaching resilience belongs primarily to parents.

What Parents Can Do and Say

Finding your spot when your child is disappointed or struggling means tapping into your empathy *while letting them have their feeling.* Here are five ways you can help your children manage their upsets by staying on your spot:

1. **First, learn to handle your own feelings about their situation.** That includes managing your own disappointment, as well as your heartache about their disappointment. Your sturdiness will inspire theirs. It lets your children know they can get through a setback when they see your steady composure and know you have confidence in them.

2. **Learn to handle *their* feelings.** When you see your child struggling with a disappointment, remember that kids learn over time how to get through difficulties with more grace and less drama. Most children partake in some variation of floor-kicking when they don't get their own way, or in lengthy sulking jags when they can't get past an upset. These reactions can overtake the whole household, and the kids who persist with these the longest are often the ones whose parents are desperate to prevent them from happening. These parents may accommodate or give in so it will end quickly, or they flinch through it—conveying the message to their children that the disappointment is indeed unbearable after all.

   Instead, accept the temporary unhappiness and unease you both feel. Learn to ride it out with confidence that your children (and you) will get through it. Stay kind and firm and on your spot so they can find you there when they are ready.

3. **Support your children's resilience.** Help them find the "Oh, well"— the understanding that if they can do something about their predicament, they should, and if they can't, then "Oh, well," it's time to move on. You can understand and have compassion for your children's current unhappiness, and at the same time believe and express confidence in their ability to get through this disappointment. You've learned over time that you win some and you lose some, and losing out is a letdown but rarely a tragedy. Remembering this will help you get out of the way of your children's opportunity to be disappointed and allow them to build resilience.

4. **Model how to overcome disappointment when you experience it.** Your children study you and are watching for behaviors they will internalize and mimic. They're trying to figure out how the world works, and they are looking to you to show them. When adults encounter disappointments or setbacks, many of us unintentionally model the very sulking, blaming, and raging in frustration that we don't like seeing in our kids. If you can demonstrate that being disappointed gives you a sad feeling that you experience (with some grace) and then move beyond, you will show your kids how resilience works and it will help them, eventually, to catch on.

5. **Remember that you already know how to do this.** Over the years as your kids have been developing skills and capacities, your courage and confidence enabled you to resist the impulse to step in and do it for them. You've let go as your wobbly kids learned to take their first steps. You held back as your children struggled with fastening buttons and tying shoelaces, knowing that tolerating their frustration was the only way they could learn those pieces of self-sufficiency. You sent them back to school when yesterday was hard for them, trusting that today was a new day and likely to be better.

These are the kinds of support your kids need from you as they navigate life's disappointments and heartbreak. We can stand by, wipe their tears, and commiserate. Most importantly, we can give them the gift of our confidence in their capacity for resilience.

Spotlights

- Kids have a disappointment muscle that needs opportunities to get exercised.

- Experience with disappointment is how kids develop confidence and resilience.

- Help your children make the best of whatever happens, instead of needing to have the best—or exactly what they want.

- When kids struggle with disappointment, don't overreact; instead, express compassion for their feelings, and confidence that they will move through it.

- Help your kids identify when a disappointing situation just needs to be accepted with an "Oh, well."

CHAPTER 10

Your Role in Your Child's School Life

School is your children's world away from home, so your involvement there needs to be right-sized and well placed: not too much and not too little, enough to be supportive without getting in their way—so they can find their own way.

How Homelife Impacts Your Child's School Life

Life at home has a huge influence on how children manage their school lives. We may not recognize whether we are preparing our kids well until we have a chance to see how they are navigating their world at school.

Sometimes our children's experiences at home support them as students, like when family life teaches them about self-reliance, consideration, waiting their turn, give and take, and making the best of things when a situation doesn't go their way.

Other times, homelife leaves children confused about how things work outside their own families. They may be inexperienced managing themselves or tuning in to others, or they may be puzzled by the social reciprocity that is needed to negotiate life in the classroom and schoolyard. Sometimes parents don't recognize that behavior we're accustomed to at home doesn't always translate well at school.

When Ethan started kindergarten, he tended to try to build relationships by punching his classmates on the arm, sitting on top of them, or encouraging a "dogpile." Ethan was confused when the other kindergarteners backed away to avoid what they considered to be an attack. In addition to being concerned about the safety of his classmates, Ethan's teacher worried that he would be unable to make friends unless he developed different ways of approaching kids so that they would be receptive to him.

Fortunately, rather than responding to Ethan's seemingly aggressive actions as "misbehavior," his teacher got curious, asked him questions, and discovered the explanation for his behavior. Ethan had three older brothers and was accustomed to interactions at home that involved a lot of rough play, so his approach to his new classmates was what he was used to doing at home. Once his teacher understood, she reached out to partner with his parents and help Ethan learn more welcome approaches to make better connections with his new friends.

Parents need to stay alert about how well their kids are managing all the variables in school life. If you find that your kids aren't managing well, then figure out if your homelife needs to include more experience and preparation for what school life asks of them, or if the teacher and others at school need more information or context to help support your children there.

When teachers present you with concerns about your child's social interactions at school, ask that they share the observations and anecdotes that led to their concerns. Once you have the full picture from them, you can add to it by sharing aspects of your child's personality or circumstances that might help frame your child's behavior. That will give the teacher a clearer picture of your child, while also helping you figure out how to support your child at home to better handle what's called for at school.

When you feel that your child is misunderstood at school, recognize that it's important to be aware of how your child is viewed by others—teachers and peers—because only then will you be able to bridge the image your child is creating at school with the kid you know at home. It is very common for children to behave differently at school than at home, as they respond to different expectations and as they try on various personas and postures.

In contrast to hearing difficult news from school, when you get feedback that seems so positive that it is unrecognizable to you—your children are more cooperative, caring, and industrious than they are at home—it might signal that your children are getting something in the school setting that could enrich family life as well: more clarity, consistency, or structure, for example.

Your Spot and School

Because our children's school experiences sometimes tap into our own, we can tend to get over-involved and step in too far or back away too much. The challenge is finding a way to be there and support your children's school life from your spot—not stepping on theirs—so their school experiences can be their own.

One sure way to notice that you're off your spot is when you catch yourself making comments like, "We have a history test on Thursday." It's actually your child who has the history test. You already had your turn at sixth grade!

Sometimes it takes a situation at school to help parents find a right-sized role in their children's classroom life.

Jayden was in third grade and her mom was carpooling her and a few friends to school in the morning. While her mother was letting the kids out at the curb, Jayden mentioned, "Oh, I had homework last night and I forgot to do it. We were supposed to make a chart."

Her mom had a huge reaction. "What?? You don't have your homework?!"

Jayden replied, "No, I forgot to bring the chart home to fill out, but it's OK; I can do it in class."

By now the other kids had left the car, and her mom said to her, "Jayden, homework is an important responsibility. You needed to have it ready for your teacher today!"

Jayden said, "No, really, Mom. It's no big deal. I'll just tell the teacher and it will be OK."

At that point, Jayden's mother was so concerned that her daughter wasn't taking her homework seriously enough that—to her child's chagrin—she insisted on parking the car and going with her to speak with the teacher.

Jayden's mom explained that Jayden had forgotten her chart and consequently hadn't done her homework, and that she only just learned about the problem as she was dropping Jayden at school.

This mother's voice must have conveyed her upset, because in an exceptionally calming tone, the teacher assured her that it was alright; then she turned to Jayden to say, "You can just do the chart in class today."

Jayden looked at her mom and said, "See, Mom, that's what I told you." Then the teacher handed Jayden the chart and suggested she start on it; she turned to Jayden's mother and asked her to come outside.

The teacher escorted Jayden's mom down the hall to the staff room, got a piece of paper from the shelf, and started writing. Jayden's mother asked, "What are you doing?"

The teacher replied, "Oh, I'm just writing a letter for Jayden's college admissions for you to hold on to. I want to let them know how conscientious her mother has been to be sure she stays on track and get into a good school."

It took Jayden's mother a moment to realize the point this teacher was making, and then she smiled and asked, "Oh. Do you think I overstepped?"

The teacher nodded gently, smiling back, and said, "Jayden knew she dropped the ball, and had a plan to talk to me to work it out. Yes, I'd say you didn't need to step in there."

Jayden's mom remembers that moment with gratitude because it was the moment when she realized these things:

- *It's Jayden's turn to do school; her mom already had her turn.*

- *Experiencing the result of not doing her homework was between Jayden and her teacher, not her mother.*

- *It was a little deal and not a big one, and Jayden was already planning to make it right.*

It became clear that Jayden's mother reacted to her own anxiety that her daughter wasn't being responsible, instead of listening to Jayden and appreciating that she actually was on top of the situation. It also became evident that Jayden's mom needed to be more thoughtful and less reactive if she was going to stay on her spot during her child's school experience.

But the most important lesson of all was that the teacher, in a kind way and with a bit of humor, helped Jayden's mother face the bittersweet fact that while the mom's intentions were good, she was being "demoted" by her child, in a positive and developmentally necessary way.

The teacher had let her know that when your children are ready to take something on, you need to be ready to let them.

Sometimes we parents have to get out of our own way to see that our kids are growing, so our role is necessarily changing—and teachers are often the ones who can help us discover that.

The Roles Teachers Play in Your Child's Development

Teachers are influential figures in the lives of children, and can be important resources for parents as well. Beyond playing an academic role, a teacher can be another adult in your child's life who acts as an "on-the-job trainer" in life skills, manners, and discovering how to be a member of a community. Teachers support your children's development in a variety of ways, including four pivotal ones:

1. Coaching children to keep track of things, learn about procedures, communicate respectfully, and do their part in the classroom setting

2. Defining in-bounds and out-of-bounds behavior for their students

3. Helping children understand the expectations for "citizenship" in the classroom and school community

4. Serving as agents of reciprocity to help kids figure out how to take turns, how their behaviors affect others, and what happens when they push against boundaries

If the messages children get at home align with what's happening at school—preparing them to manage what will be asked of them—they tend to have a much smoother school experience. The key to synchronizing messages at home and school is partnering with your children's teachers.

Teachers tend to work with kids of the same age group year after year and become field experts on that specific developmental stage of childhood. So while you're attuned to who your children are and what distinguishes them as unique individuals, teachers are in a position of expertise to talk about your children relative to other students of the same age.

Teachers can help you understand what attitudes, academic skills, and social behaviors are in range developmentally, and whether your perspectives about your children fit into that range. This is valuable information that would be very hard for you to gauge on your own.

Teachers can also offer a window into your child's world outside of home that you can't see. It's typical for children to behave differently with parents than with others. A teacher's observations help you understand what areas are going well for your child and where some additional clarity or support might be needed from you. Your child's teachers may also surprise you by sharing that your child exhibits some wonderful traits and skills that haven't shown up at home yet. When it comes to our kids' growing capacities, sometimes parents are the last to know!

It's easy to hear the positives; naturally, the teacher's concerns or critical observations may be less welcome. As a result, some parents dismiss the teacher's observations, overlook important cues and messages, and miss out on the benefits a teacher can offer about supporting the child's school life.

At the start of the year, Christopher's assignment during a second-grade unit on ancient Egypt was to bring in an old stuffed animal from home to wrap as a "mummy," which the students would unwrap at the end of the unit. However, Christopher didn't want to part with one of his collection of many, many stuffed animals, so his mom bought him a brand new one to avoid any upset.

Christopher's teacher told his parents that all of his classmates had brought stuffed animals from home that they already owned, except Christopher (whose new animal still had the price tags attached), and she was concerned about Christopher's inflexibility—that he couldn't manage to do what all of the other children were doing. Christopher's parents explained that he had especially deep feelings, and they were used to making these kinds of exceptions for him. So the teacher relented and let him use his new animal.

Later in the year, Christopher's parents were thrown by his refusal to go to his best friend's birthday party. When Sheri asked him why he didn't want to go, Christopher explained that it was because he knew the party venue had only one chair with arms—the chair for the special birthday child—and insisted that he would attend only if he could sit in a chair with arms.

Relieved to hear that was the issue, his mom immediately offered to Christopher, "We have a folding chair with arms; I can bring it to the party for you!"

Sheri explained, "This is exactly what is getting in Christopher's way of figuring out how to go with the flow. Christopher hasn't learned how to cope if he has to sit in a chair without arms or spend a week without one of his toys. As the teacher was trying to tell you, you're giving him the message that he can't manage what the rest of the kids are managing, and it's beginning to limit him."

Christopher expected the same contouring to his personal needs out in the world that happened at home. Of course it's different when there is a classroom (or birthday party) full of other children to consider, and Christopher didn't have the confidence or capability to manage when he had to make adjustments. The pattern his teacher recognized and shared with his parents had begun to resonate for them, though they initially missed the chance to partner with her.

Sometimes it takes parents a while to absorb and recognize feedback from teachers.

Thea's parents brought her to Sheri when Thea was a high school student, exasperated because Thea was endlessly oppositional and refused to cooperate both at school and with them.

Sheri discovered that when Thea was in preschool, her teacher had voiced this very concern to her parents: "When the whole group of children is going left, Thea always goes right," to which the parents took offense and replied, "We applaud our daughter's individuality and independence."

Fast-forwarding to high school, Thea's parents still appreciated her determination and strong sense of self, but they wished they had paid attention to what the preschool teacher was telling them: Their daughter had independence down, but she still needed to learn how to be cooperative and responsive to others in settings where she wasn't in charge.

Thea's parents missed the opportunity to partner with her preschool teacher and help their daughter learn when and how to be "just like everybody else" by joining in. It was a lot tougher to help Thea learn those social skills as a teen, after more years of the same patterning. As they struggled with the realization, her parents were able to identify a number of times when teachers gave feedback along the way that they hadn't accepted.

Teachers may also be in a position to notice when there is a difference in how a child behaves based on the setting.

Elijah was a seventh grader for whom his parents felt they had to do everything, all the time. They nudged him repeatedly to do chores, as he wouldn't do anything on his own or the first time he was asked. Every night was a struggle getting him to close his computer and get to bed, and then another struggle to get him up and going in the morning.

Elijah's teacher saw a different Elijah, and she told Sheri a story about his exemplary behavior during a school field trip. He demonstrated leadership, impressing his teachers with his initiative and helpfulness with adults and the other kids. He was one of the most attentive, engaged, and respectful students on the trip.

When the bus came back to school, however, the teacher observed that the minute Elijah's mom showed up, suddenly he couldn't find his duffel bag, he couldn't lift it himself, and he complained loudly and insistently that he was starving. The teacher was stunned by the transformation. His mom, meanwhile, immediately accommodated Elijah by carrying his bag and cajoling him with the promise of stopping for a snack on the way home.

During their conferences, the teacher shared her observations with Elijah's parents, both from the trip and of Elijah's reunion with his mom, and it gave them a window to the Elijah they didn't get to see. To their credit, his parents were receptive to the feedback, and came to their next session with Sheri ready to talk about the ways that they had underestimated Elijah and were unwittingly holding him back from being more self-reliant.

Partnering with Teachers to Support Your Child

In the same way that teachers provide a window for parents, you can provide teachers with important insights to help them appreciate your children's less-obvious needs as well as their observable talents.

- **The Past:** Be sure the teacher has relevant information about your child's learning and social experiences both in and out of school—including her strengths and challenges—which may or may not be evident in school records.

- **The Present:** Keep the teacher updated with any recent or unfolding circumstances that might impact your child's behavior or engagement at school (for instance, a grandparent recently died, or one parent began traveling for work so the household went out of sync).

- **Perceptions:** When your child reports being upset about repeated incidents at school that go beyond his ability to manage, give his teacher feedback from the child's perspective—with the goal of clearing up confusion, rather than running interference for your child.

  > **Instead of:** *"My son said that you wouldn't let him be excused for his doctor's appointment, and that just isn't right."*
  >
  > **Try:** *"I want to share something confusing that my son said to me, so we can compare notes and figure this out."*

Approach teachers from a place of being on the same side, sharing a common goal to support your child's well-being and development.

- **Assume Goodwill:** When you meet with a teacher about concerns, lead with curiosity rather than reproach. When teachers feel that their viewpoint is welcome, it sets a tone of collaboration.

  > **Instead of:** *"Why was my daughter the only one who got in trouble when other kids were also involved in the playground incident yesterday?"*
  >
  > **Try:** *"I realize that I may not have gotten the whole story from my daughter, so can you help me understand what happened between the girls on the swings and how it was handled?"*

Not surprisingly, children are not always reliable reporters; once the teacher explains, it may clear up your concern. If not, you can ask questions and provide the teacher with more information about your child's perspective and responses.

- **Respect Your Role and the Teacher's:** Describe your concern to the teacher rather than posing a solution. Assume that the teacher has the skills to address the concern on their own terms, rather than crossing the line to tell them what to do.

Instead of: *"My daughter needs to sit at a different table. Her table is filled with noisy kids who aren't serious students, and I want her moved to a table with more high-achieving students."*

Try: *"My daughter has been reporting that she finds her tablemates very distracting. She has difficulty hearing you because they are talking with each other, and it's hard for her to concentrate when they call out or get in and out of their seats during math and writing."*

Now the teacher has what is needed to understand your concern and can figure out and share a plan to address your daughter's distress. If it falls short of what you hoped for, help your child devise strategies for managing upsetting situations. It may turn out that learning to handle these kinds of circumstances is a more important lesson than the one that's missed at the front of the classroom. Of course, if these efforts don't support a more helpful direction, follow up with the teacher and talk about other steps to take.

Maintaining Boundaries between School and Home

School is your children's own world away from home, and they need the space (and your confidence in their sturdiness) to be their own people there. When you get overly involved in their school world, you interrupt important lessons they are learning about self-reliance, self-care, and interpersonal relations. They need to be on their own, in their world, to benefit from those lessons.

This is where the "not too much, not too little" part comes in. Many kids (especially younger children) enjoy it when their parents participate in their classrooms, drive on field trips, and show up to help with special events at school. There's an art to participating at school in a way that lets your children feel your support without intruding on their world.

Often, the biggest obstacle to the parent-kid-teacher triad running in a smooth and cooperative manner is when parents, teachers, and children lose track of boundaries and struggle to remember who belongs where.

When a teacher says, *"You should limit your son's out-of-school activities so he can get his homework done,"* that teacher is actually stepping on your toes about managing homelife, instead of identifying her concern about his homework and asking for your support to address it. It's the teacher's role to let you know that homework completion is a problem, and it's your role to determine how to address it at home.

To do: When you get teacher feedback about your child, be sure to ask the teacher to be clear about what he is observing, and what he, as a teacher, would like to see happen. You can then offer ways you can support that. For example, if the concern is that your son's homework is often incomplete, it was in the teacher's court to remind the student that he should turn in completed work. If that doesn't get results and the teacher is turning to you for help, it's up to you to find a way to make sure your child has the time and support at home to complete homework.

● ● ●

When a parent tells a teacher, *"You need to use a different math program that's more engaging,"* that parent is stepping over the line into the teacher's territory, in the same way that a teacher would be by prescribing how you should parent your child.

To do: You can raise a concern about how your child is responding to the math curriculum, along with questions (rather than criticisms) you have about the teacher's approach. It's your place as a parent to ask for clarity and reassurance, so the teacher will be more likely to be receptive to your concerns and welcome your feedback as a basis for discussion. Teachers are inclined to be responsive when they feel you are looking to partner with them to support your child's learning experience.

● ● ●

When a child says to her parent, *"You have to help me with my paper right now; it's already overdue!"* she doesn't understand which one of you is accountable for homework and how to approach people when she wants help with something that is her responsibility.

To do: Help her get clear about this. *"If you're asking for my help, please just let me know that rather than telling me I 'have to.'"* The reason you may need to deal with this over and over again is that somehow it was communicated to your child that homework is your concern, rather than hers (perhaps by saying things like *"We have a history test on Thursday!"*).

Thinking twice about roles and boundaries will help you stay on your spot to find that balance between "not too much and not too little" with your children and their teachers.

Homework: Whose Business Is It?

When it comes to homework, it can be challenging to stay on your spot as you consider the somewhat delicate matter of clarifying how much involvement is not too much and not too little. Because homework bridges school and home, and everyone in the parent-kid-teacher triad is involved, boundaries can get blurry. Here's a way to keep it all straight:

- The student is the one who needs to do homework. It is their responsibility.

- The teacher is the supervisor, the one who assigns the work and the person to whom your child answers about it.

- Homework issues are primarily between a student and the teacher.

- Unless you are asked by the teacher to do more, a parent's role in regard to homework involves the following:

  o Communicate your values about learning and doing schoolwork to your child.

  o Let your child know where homework fits into the scheme of routines and activities at home.

- Provide the time and a suitable space at home for your child to do homework (noting that some kids need quiet solitude, like a bedroom, and others need company and oversight, like the kitchen table while dinner prep is going on).

- Be available to help as a "consultant" (not a supervisor!) who can be hired—and fired—by your child as needed.

Remember That Homework Belongs to Your Children

Homework is your children's first ongoing responsibility outside of the home, and it's important to their development that they own it. The whole home-work experience—learning how to show what they know and facing what they don't—is your children's to experience. You already had your turn.

Many of the difficult dynamics parents encounter with their kids about homework emerge from the illusion that homework is a power struggle between children and parents. It goes better when your children are allowed to develop an internal sense that they are accountable to someone beyond their parents for schoolwork. If the power struggle is happening, step aside—although it may be hard to do—and let your children's teachers follow through to help realign expectations. Your children's assignments are given and should be over-seen by their teachers; you're just on board to provide support if needed. That said, there are times when a child's resistance to homework is a face-saving signal that they're struggling with a "can't" rather than a "won't." If you're concerned about this, check in with the teacher and compare notes, and get additional help.

Communicate a Mindset about Education

As in all areas of parenting, the messages you give your children influence their attitudes and behavior. What you communicate to your children about how you hold the importance of education, and about what you expect of them as students, guides how they approach learning and doing schoolwork.

When you overstep your role and push for outcomes, this pressure creates anxiety rather than motivation. You want to inspire a love and excitement for learning that comes from within, rather than a stress response to pressure that comes from outside. The latter leads to strain and relationship struggles, while the former is a gift that enriches and can last their lifetime.

Provide Time and Space for Homework

Part of supporting your child in school is being sure that family time and other activities are "homework friendly." In the same way that households need to accommodate parents' work schedules, they also need to accommodate children's school and homework time. Your role is to support and provide scaffolding (a place to work, limitations on distractions, time parameters, and support for time management) so your children can do their homework. You are responsible for creating the environment that lets homework get done, but you are not responsible for doing it.

Be Available to Help as a "Consultant"

Since homework is your child's job and supervising it is the teacher's, you can be available as a "consultant." Your child would have hiring power (asking for your help) and firing power ("I want to do this myself"). And, of course, you can offer to make your services available ("I'm happy to help edit your rough draft if you'd like" or "You seem to be struggling with that math assignment; would you like some help?"). Like any good consultant, you can also decline if the working conditions are too rough ("I don't like the way you are talking to me, so I'm going to take a break from working on this with you," and "I know it's frustrating and I'm glad to help you again when you are able to use a kinder tone with me").

When your child doesn't do assigned homework, it might seem unclear whether it's your issue to deal with or the teacher's. Further, when your child says, "Leave me alone; it's my homework and not yours," or when your older student announces at bedtime that unfinished homework due tomorrow requires a delay in bedtime, you might get confused about your responsibilities.

- If you're aware that your child hasn't completed homework, as a consultant with time-management skills, you can provide a prompt: *"I just want to remind you that this is due tomorrow."* If the assignment is incomplete, it will be the teacher's place to address that with your child. It's really important for your children to experience the results of what they do or don't do, in the place where that belongs: with the teacher, at school.

- When your children ask to be left alone because their homework is their business and not yours, they're right. They need to understand that it is indeed theirs. You can back off from pushing or worrying when your children are rightfully letting you know that you're trying to assume responsibility that should be theirs. Sometimes kids will assure their parents that their homework is done when it isn't. If that happens, first clarify what took place. Did your child misunderstand or forget an assignment? Was she misleading you to avoid doing the work? Once you understand the issue, you can address the need for more oversight (by helping with organization or tracking) or address the honesty concern (by double-checking until trust is restored and reliability is in place)—while still keeping responsibility for homework in your child's court.

- When your older student stays up very late to finish homework, you again need to clarify your role and find your spot. There's no single answer in this example; maybe you gave prompts all weekend that your child ignored, and the homework is now spilling past a bedtime to which you want to hold firm. Or it could be that your child may be doing the best job possible and it's just one of those assignments and it's going to be one of those nights. Or perhaps you are discovering that your child has chronic challenges with organization and time management that need to be understood and supported. Take the time to assess what happened, find your spot, get clear on your priority in this moment, and decide what you might want to put into place to address this recurring issue.

Your Homework Checklist

To get your footing regarding your role in your child's homework, here's a checklist to help:

1. Let your children lead—let them do what they can do, first. Remember, it's their assignment, not yours (or "ours").

2. Be sure to encourage your child to ask for help. Beyond learning math or sentence structure, kids also need to learn how to reach out for help and not assume adults will simply anticipate their needs without the child taking an active role in making it happen. You want your kids to learn to self-advocate, and that includes asking for support when things get difficult.

3. When your children do ask for help, rather than just jumping in, clarify what they don't understand (a word definition, a math sequence) and try to determine what support they might need (hints about what similar words mean, or a reminder about the formula's first step). Then offer the help that will allow them to complete the assignment.

4. If they still struggle with it, encourage them to talk to their teacher about what is so hard, but resist the temptation to do the work for them. When you help your children excessively with their homework, the teacher won't be able to identify what your child understands, what your child's needs are, and what still needs to be learned. In turn, this limits the teacher's ability to support your child in the near term, which often causes problems in the longer term. What's more, encouraging children to talk to the teacher about their needs helps build agency and self-advocacy skills and promotes their relationship with their teacher.

5. If the issues are ongoing, share your specific observations of your child's struggles with the teacher, and ask for the teacher's observations so you both have a fuller picture.

If your child's homework challenges match difficulties the teacher observes at school as well, additional support may be required. The more opportunity your children have to take on their own work and display learning (or learning challenges) to the teacher, and the more two-way communication you and the teacher maintain, the sooner any special issues will be identified and your children will get the help they need.

Your role is to be sure that your children own their homework, that teachers have the information they need about your children to be effective with them in class, and that you find your place at your children's side at home, supporting them rather than taking an authoritative role with homework.

Remember to be aware of inadvertent messages you may unintentionally convey, such as when you complain about the quantity or nature of your children's homework or disclose unfavorable opinions of their teachers. While having a deliberate and frank discussion may help your child manage a challenging relationship with a teacher, indirect comments and inuendo can leave your child with an undefined unease about the teacher and about school, making it difficult to thrive there.

While homework may test your ability to stay on your spot, it's also a daily reminder that your children have their own world, with their own experiences and responsibilities, and it gives you a very concrete way to continuously practice being there for your child in ways that are not too little and not too much.

Spotlights

- Ensure that homelife prepares your children for the expectations and responsibilities they will need to manage at school.

- Give messages that encourage a positive attitude about learning and education.

- Partner with teachers by collaborating to support your child's learning and school life.

- Homework is between students and teachers; provide your kids with the time and space, along with any support they may need, to do their assignments on their own.

- School is primarily your children's world, so keep your place in their school life right-sized: not too much, not too little.

CHAPTER 11

Kids, Screens, and Family Life

"**B**eing home" isn't what it used to be.
    Neither is "being at work," "being with friends," or "being together as a family." Where we are, who we are with, and what we are doing is neither obvious nor straightforward anymore. Technology has changed that.

In many ways, technology has enriched family life: making pickups and drop-offs easier, supporting planning and changes in plans, letting parents who are apart from kids still help with homework, keeping grandparents who live at a distance connected to grandkids, keeping tabs on children's and parents' whereabouts, providing access and coordination when it comes to family emergencies. And much more.

That said, with technology in our homes, we've had to readjust our perspectives about what "being at home" means, in part because the lines between life at home and what was life-outside-of-home have become blurred:

- "Family time" at home may very well include a teenager virtually hanging out with a friend or a myriad of friends on texts, chats, social media, video conferencing, or gaming. It may also include a parent who is constantly checking work emails, reviewing documents, or attending a meeting online. The dinner table often doubles as a computer station, and meals may be joined by uninvited (and perhaps undetected) guests on devices. Closing the front door no longer means "It's just us here."

- Work is not office bound, and we're never fully away from it anymore in a 24/7 connected world. And even when we are in an office or traveling for work, we are never fully disengaged from home now that our umbilical cord has gone wireless. Family members can connect with each other at nearly any time, to and from nearly anywhere.

- A child's home, school, and social lives blend together with technology, often simultaneously. The saying "There's a time and place for everything" has been replaced with "It's always the time and place for anything."

And yet, at the heart of things, nothing has changed.

If the digital era seems to have a life of its own, dictating the course of your family culture, testing your values, hijacking your routines and plans . . . it's probably because you haven't found your spot yet in this area of everyday parenting. Your role as a parent, including how you relate, set boundaries, encourage manners, instill values, set limits—stays the same in either language, analog or digital. For generations, as children and teens walked out the door, parents have asked them, "Where are you going? Who are you going to be with? When will you be back?"

Those same questions still apply as your kids head off to play video games or post on social media sites. The digital world calls for the same parenting oversight that's relevant in the physical world.

Relating

Your first step in relating to your kids in a positive, supportive way is learning about and appreciating their digital world.

Most children have a natural and strong connection with technology, in the same way that they have relationships with their friends, school life, sports, and other activities. Technology is simply a given for most kids; to relate to your children regarding devices, you need to understand and appreciate their relationship to screens.

Your relationship with your children is at the center of helping them manage their digital world. If you can relate to your children's online life, you can figure out how to be on their side in helping them manage it.

- If your children are more excited about screens and technology than you are, and they are more familiar than you are with activities and sites, think about how you can get them to engage you so you can become educated about their on-screen world and develop more understanding and an appreciation for their online interests.

- If you're already fluent in technology and know your way around their digital interests, you can relate to their enthusiasm with both sensitivity and legitimized authority as you monitor their on-screen activities. If you understand the draw and the drawbacks of particular social media, games, and sites, then you can openly discuss the basis for your decisions about their freedoms and limits.

Navigating your kids' digital life starts with understanding and accepting it. Before you take steps to monitor, limit, and control your children's screen use, you need to figure out what's working and what isn't, get the information you need to make the best call, and communicate clearly with your kids about where you stand and what you expect from them when it comes to technology.

- *"Help me understand how this game/social media site works. Can you show me? What do you like about it?"*

- *"Here's the part I like about what you're doing online, and here's the part I'm concerned about. I'd like to figure out a way for you to get to do what matters to you that avoids the part I'm uncomfortable with."*

- *"I know that you want to spend some time today playing your game/hanging out online. Let's figure out where that will fit into the family plans we have."*

For some kids, just recognizing that parents are interested and want to engage with and oversee what they do online will nudge them to keep their activities more wholesome. Others may search for workarounds to keep you from discovering their off-limits activities. This is just one example of why your relationship with your kids, along with your clarity about values and boundaries, needs to stay front and center when it comes to screens.

Boundaries and Privacy

The infinite connectivity that technology provides has complicated how, why, and when we communicate. Just because we can communicate digitally doesn't always mean we should. In fact, there are plenty of times when digital messages are inappropriate, such as . . .

- when a parent is busy at work and gets texts or calls that demand an immediate response from partner or kids about issues that can wait until they are together.

- when there are relationship concerns that need to be addressed that warrant the personal exchange of a conversation rather than a text or email.

- when someone sends us a text or email to which we have a strong reaction, and we immediately forward it to other family members or friends because it's so easy to react.

Today there are virtually no constraints on anyone's ability to cross boundaries to be in touch, to pass information along, or to irreversibly express sentiments before taking the time to process them. There are very few external limitations that require us to think before we publish our thoughts, to work through and perhaps overcome our feelings without immediate discharge.

Those restraints need to come from within, and especially for our children who are born in the digital age, they need to be taught and modeled.

Perhaps hardest for all of us is learning to withstand our feelings when we have an urge to connect that may not be timely or appropriate, or considerate of the needs of others. Encourage your kids to think twice, to be deliberate in their communications, and to sort out who belongs in a given conversation, on a given topic, at a given moment, and with respect to other boundaries.

This leads us to the issue of privacy. Privacy isn't what it used to be, either.

The rapid expansion of technology has shifted our notions of privacy. For instance:

- While at one time it would have been considered intrusive to read your child's private journal, being aware of what he's doing online (where nothing is truly private) is now considered "responsible parenting."

- Personal feelings or thoughts are published as soon as they are felt or thought and before their impact is considered, so what we communicate about ourselves and know from others may not have been wisely shared.

- Comments that might have been expressed in fleeting conversations between two or a few are now indelibly posted, for all to see online.

- The ease with which messages (and parts of messages out of context) can be forwarded, rebroadcast, or misdirected also illustrates the public nature of everything we do online.

Digital communication has dramatically changed what kids (and adults) can expect to keep private. The mixed blessing of transparency that technology brings is here to stay. That means your children need to be educated about the impact of what they express and access online. They also need to understand that because the impact can be beyond what they may fully grasp, you will be keeping an eye on it.

This is where your relationship with them comes into the picture.

If you are familiar with and understand your children's digital activities, you'll have the knowledge to be credible when you guide them about what they encounter and contribute online. Further, if you refrain from using punishment to manage them, and instead have a relationship where your kids feel safe about being honest with you—knowing that if they cross lines, you will help them understand that and make it right—they will be more accepting of your supervision and monitoring.

> *"We feel that you're ready to have your own phone, and we're OK with you being on a couple of the social media and gaming sites you're interested in. We want to be able to see your postings and to have your passwords so we can check in from time to time."*

Some kids will take that in stride; for others it will be the beginning of a conversation about "why." If you've found your spot with regard to social media and gaming before that discussion, you can stay on your spot throughout.

> *"I noticed that you used some pretty harsh language in your post. While your friends might be fine with that, their parents may not be, and that could make it hard on your friendships. Be thoughtful about the effect it has on all the people who might read this, not just the person you're writing it to."*

Knowing that your comment will be followed up by monitoring is likely to give it legs. If it doesn't, and your children don't take your guidance seriously, they might not be ready for social media and gaming sites yet.

As technology slices through barriers to communicating, we need to intentionally establish boundaries to help us (parents and kids alike) think twice before we act. Our shared goal is to verify who belongs in which conversations, to take pause when we need time to think about boundaries, and to be thoughtful no matter how easy and tempting it is to reply, post, or hit "send."

Manners

We are well into the digital era, but social etiquette is still analog.

Our cultural conventions haven't been able to keep up with the pace of technology. There isn't yet a common protocol or set of manners for using our devices. In grocery stores and restaurants, during family drives and at dinner tables, adults and kids annoy and offend one another with their screen behaviors, but still there are no clear guidelines for socially acceptable use of technology.

Most families lack a shared understanding about when using technology is OK and when it's not. Here are some guidelines for coming to your own set of family tech manners:

- Establish an understanding about the use of devices in various settings and during certain segments of family life: at meals, on car rides, during conversations, at bedtime. Be sure that you are on your spot about what you want and that you're able to follow through (for example, have your kids dock their phones elsewhere before going to their rooms at bedtime)—and that you stick with the tech policies yourself!

- Be prepared to make exceptions to your policies, because things come up (checking your phone for an important text about your cousin in the hospital, your daughter coordinating a meeting place with her friend, and so on). Distinguish those moments as exceptions, and then get back into your pattern as soon as possible.

- Notice when something bothers or offends you and describe the problem (*"I'm finding it distracting when you check your phone while we're talking"*), rather than condemning your kid. Remember, our culture does not have widely established ethics, mores, and standards when it comes to tech use, so rather than relating to it as if your child has violated a well-known general understanding of good manners (as in forgetting to say "thank you" or interrupting without saying "excuse me"), identify the specific tech issue and ask for what you want: *"Please don't check your phone while we're having a conversation."*

Most families can point to times when the "digital manners" of one family member offended another. A family Sheri was seeing had a disagreement about digital manners at the dinner table.

The family was having dinner, and all were engaged in a lively conversation, when they veered into a point of disagreement about a historical fact. They went back and forth a bit, and then the dad got up to get his tablet, bring it to the table, and look up the details.

Mom was offended and said, "Hey, we have a no-devices-at-the-dinner-table rule, and you're setting a bad example."

To this, Dad replied, "But we value good conversation at the dinner table, and this will help us answer the question and get on with our discussion."

Both were arguing for something wholesome, one by keeping a boundary about screens and the other by leaning in to use technology for what he saw as the family's benefit.

This example illustrates the ways in which technology can both complicate and support family life—in the end, it's not the technology, but the family's values, priorities, and sensibilities that lead to constructive or contentious outcomes.

In this case, both parents were trying to hold a family value; they just went about it in different ways. Sheri helped them clarify that they were actually on the same page. While Dad was more tech savvy, and Mom was nostalgic for tradition, they both realized that the heart of the matter was the quality of their dinner time as a family.

Mom was able to agree that bringing in the tablet to clarify the disagreement did allow the conversation to continue and actually enriched it, and Dad was able to see her point about the potential slippery slope and not giving mixed messages to the kids. He promised to clarify exceptions, and to explain that they were in the service of the family value of staying connected at the table.

In addition to mealtimes, one of the most common venues for the clash between manners and technology is inside the family car. While parents of young kids welcome the entertainment of screens to make a long road trip lower maintenance and more pleasant, often local car trips become tense when unspoken boundaries are broken by kids (or adults) using technology.

From a manners standpoint, texting or watching a video from the back or passenger's seat is just like making a phone call or picking up a book. It separates the user from others in the car. Parents need to consider how they feel about that, to determine what they want the "culture" of their car rides to be, and to inform their kids clearly. For example: "I know your dad doesn't mind when you're immersed in your phone while he's driving, but I do because I'd like your company. Unless there's something important, I'd like the car to be a 'no-phone zone' when I drive."

And of course, there's always room for accommodation. Just as kids are taught to make requests when an intrusion is anticipated in other circumstances, doing the same here shows their intention to be considerate and may win them an exception: "Would you mind if I use my phone while we're in the car?"

Try to get clarity on what you would like the digital culture of your family to be, starting with manners, and find your spot so you can manage these moments with thoughtfulness and conviction.

Screens and Limits

While many families used to watch screens together (TV and videos) as a family activity on weekends, families now find that their children's social world is so screen-oriented that to help balance their children's lives, family activities need to be non-screen. The key is finding the appropriate balance of online and offline engagement for each child.

To find that balance, provide direction for your kids by pointing them toward activities that they don't do often enough, rather than just limiting screen-focused activities that become overly consuming. Since the heart of the matter for most parents regarding "too much screen time" is that kids' lives get out of balance, then instead of having repeated power struggles over "screen time," it makes sense and is friendlier to address the balance issue instead. Helping them learn balance also involves being sure children set aside time for family interaction, homework, exercise, chores, and sleep.

One thing to consider as you set screen time limits is that there are different types of acceptable online activities that kids do:

- **Constructive activities:** doing homework, learning coding and engineering, creating art, developing media, organizing an event, researching an acceptable topic of interest, or reading the news

- **Leisure activities:** playing games (alone or with others) or watching videos for pure entertainment

- **Social activities:** connecting (via conversation or sharing photos or links, sometimes through a game or media-building site) with friends, classmates, relatives, and others

Playing with friends (role-playing, construction projects, dress-up, ball-games) doesn't necessarily require kids to go outside or to get together with other kids to play; they can do it from the couch or their bedroom. For many children today, screen activities rather than physical ones are the way they play and bond.

In the same way that some parents may want kids to take a break from physical activity to do something more restful or mind-engaging, others need to be sure their children get a break from screens to get exercise and fresh air.

The best part of using a relationship basis to get on your spot and set limits is that instead of applying a rigid structure, you can take into account the place technology and screens have in your child or teen's life. It also allows you to consider your values and needs, and use the same "operating principles" for your children that you hold for your own technology usage, rather than setting up rules that you're bound to break yourself. For example:

- Keep the role of screens in your family right-sized. Screen time can have its place in family life, just as meals, homework, bedtime, and sports practice have theirs. Consider technology as just another dimension of day-to-day living. This allows you to keep your approach to handling screens integral to managing other aspects of family life rather than making it a separate battleground, which could help prevent heated exchanges about screen time from overtaking homelife.

    Addressing screen time guidance or limits should be the same as addressing the importance of agreements, time commitments, or responsibilities in general. When time on the screen begins to surpass staying connected with family, getting enough sleep, or attending to responsibilities, it's the imbalance that is the issue, not a power struggle about screens. The best way to keep screens from becoming too central in a household is to address the areas of family life that need more attention.

- Rather than, *"You're spending too much time on that screen; you need to get off in ten minutes,"* try saying, *"In ten minutes we're heading out the door for soccer practice"* (or *"It's dinner time,"* or *"It's family game night,"* or *"It's bedtime"*). Many parents focus on what they don't want their kids to do, and to the kids, it feels like criticism of them and of an activity they value. Instead, focus on what you *do* want them to do, and be sure it genuinely matters to you.

- Understand that just as you may break a promise to your partner or children to be off your laptop in five minutes when you're "just finishing up an email," your kids can't time to the minute the end of a game, a posting exchange, or other activities online. Unlike broadcast television or movies that have discrete time frames, segments of online activity are harder to pin down. Be compassionate about that, and give looser but contained frames for screen boundaries:

  - *"Just one game."*

  - *"OK, you can get online for a while, but we're going out to lunch at noon, so you'll have a hard stop then."*

  - *"It's your sister's turn to be on the computer, so find a stopping place within the next fifteen minutes."*

The key to setting limits around screens is the same with setting limits in general. It starts with being on your spot and having clarity about what matters and what you expect.

Technology changes our lives rapidly, but common sense, human values, and family culture are a parent's North Star, no matter whether you are in real time or virtual space.

Spotlights

- Understanding your kids' digital life will help you find your spot about what they do on screens and how much time they spend doing it.

- Keep your relationship central so your children will be receptive to your advice and limits about screens.

- Encourage the other activities you want your kids to do (homework, outdoor play, family time, bedtime) rather than criticizing their screen time.

- Since there are no widely accepted standards for digital manners, create your own policies for when, where, and how your family uses devices.

- Focus on helping your kids establish a wholesome balance of interests and activities, both on- and offline.

CHAPTER 12

Raising Kids with Character

Little eyes are watching, and little ears are listening.

From your children's first days, your everyday choices, comments, responses, and behaviors inform their emerging attitudes and belief systems. Your children's character development starts with yours.

Your Influence on Character Development

Ethics and values are embedded in every aspect of your life with your kids, and are continuously communicated through your words and actions. The priorities you set each day send messages about what matters to you—how you see yourself and your role, how you value your time and the time of others.

- How you balance work and family communicates your boundaries, your have-tos and want-tos.

- How you handle everyday interactions with family members and others sends messages about how you feel people should be treated.

- Whether you mean what you say, and keep your word when you give it, signal how you value credibility and reliability.

- How you manage conflicts between your children conveys your views about what is right and wrong, and which ways of expressing themselves have your approval or disapproval.

- Who's in charge of what in your household, how that is expressed, and what responses are welcome or discouraged signal to your children your approach to authority, leadership, cooperation, and collaboration.

- How talking and listening happen in your household guides kids' ideas about how conversations should go, whether what they say matters to you, whether what you say should matter to them, and how you expect people to regard each other.

The messages conveyed in your behavior fills day-to-day homelife with signals about your character and the character traits you value. Your kids absorb their observations as they construct their own values, attitudes, and behaviors.

Some of the absorption is immediate, and other observations are stored and applied in the future when they become relevant. You may have noticed yourself doing this, for example, when you started a family and discovered yourself replicating some of your parents' values and approaches that you hadn't been aware you held so closely—until you found yourself putting them into play with your own children.

Most of the messages parents send intentionally do a good job of reflecting their values. Think about the powerful messages embedded in these everyday parenting comments:

- *"Once I get dinner in the oven, I'll come play with you."* (Business comes before pleasure, and we tend to responsibilities in a way that leaves time for enjoyment.)

- *"We need to hurry so we are on time and our friends don't have to wait for us."* (We value others' time and their feelings.)

- *"No hitting! You can use your words to tell your brother to stop, or come to us for help."* (There are ways to take care of yourself that don't cause harm to others. We want you to use those ways.)

But the unintended messages about values that you convey can surprise you when they are reflected in your children's attitudes and behaviors as their emerging character traits.

When Anthony came home from school upset one day, he reported to his parents that it really bothered him that he was not the best reader in his first-grade class. His parents responded the way many of us would: "That's OK, sweetheart. You may not be the best reader, but you are the best at other things, like skiing and drawing."

On the surface, it seems to be a fine response, as we all have our challenges and strengths. But in terms of character development, the operative word here is "best," which sent a powerful message to Anthony.

His parents used that word often: "Anthony doesn't really enjoy skiing, although he's the best at it among his friends. He took a big leap forward when we took him to the best ski resort with the best-groomed runs, bought him the best skis, and hired the best instructor there."

The message they meant to give was about the efforts they've made to support Anthony in an activity they thought he could enjoy, given that others had been so challenging for him. However, what came across loud and clear to Anthony was this: What matters the most is having and being the best.

This was not a message his parents intended to give, and if asked, they would have said that it absolutely does not reflect their values. While they were both driven and achievement-oriented in their careers, as parents they did not intend to encourage the sense of pressure they both struggled to overcome. Yet, they were doing just that. They were not conscious of what they were communicating, nor how their son would internalize their language and actions.

So they were surprised and confused when his teacher reported that Anthony was constantly competing with and correcting his classmates, and that he was devastated when his own answers weren't right or when his team lost a game during PE class. The teacher was, in effect, calling into question Anthony's budding character and values. Anthony's parents didn't realize that while they were trying to discourage this mindset in their son, they were unwittingly promoting it.

Once they were aware of this, they made very deliberate efforts to be sure that their communication lined up with the values they actually wanted to impart. They changed their message so that instead of telling Anthony, "You may not be the best reader but you're the best at other things," they said, "Don't worry, son, everybody learns differently. Becoming a good reader happens sooner for some children and later for others. You'll see."

They shifted their language in other areas, too, mindful that he was paying attention. Instead of "This place is the best for vacation," they'd say, "We like it here very much." Indeed, being thoughtful about the messages their word choice imparted became one of their parenting values.

Still, like Anthony's parents, many parents are motivated to want their children to be the very best, and they make this goal explicit in their parenting. But in their efforts to inspire their kids toward achievements, ambitious parents may also convey additional messages unknowingly:

- *"We love you more when you're on top."*
- *"Effort only matters when you win or succeed."*
- *"Your accomplishments are important to my well-being as a parent."*

These aren't necessarily messages you intend to give as a parent, but they can come across when you're not thoughtful about the way you express your encouragement, what captures your attention and involvement, or your reactions to your children's performances and experiences. Similarly, we give unintended messages about truth when our children hear us fudge or misrepresent facts to avoid a conflict or disruption, or about integrity when we get defensive instead of owning up to a misstep or mistake. Be aware of your motivations, communicate as clearly and deliberately as you can, and notice when your children respond, as Anthony was doing, to a message you didn't mean to send.

Character Messages That Support Your Kids

Childhood is an open field filled with opportunities and obstacles that build and test your child's emerging character. Day-to-day life at home, at school, in sports, and in the neighborhood, along with pointed input from adults, siblings, peers, and media, all add to the mix of information, observations, experiences, thoughts, and feelings that contribute to a child's developing character.

Input from many sources and the ups and downs of life inevitably shape your child's character. As the most important influence in their lives, how you respond to surprises, challenges, and setbacks sends powerful messages to your children about what those experiences mean and how to manage them. While parents tend to focus on the effect that events will have on their children, they often miss that it's not what happens to us in life that matters, *but what we make of each situation* that counts.

This is one of the most important messages you can offer your children to build a positive sense of themselves and of what's possible in their lives. Help your kids learn to respond to life experiences in a way that aligns with who they want to be, how they want to act, and what impact they want to have in the world. This will help build their confidence, competence, and character.

Olivia made friends with a new fifth-grader who was shy and had been picked on at her previous school. When Olivia saw her new friend getting made fun of during recess one morning, Olivia approached the girls who were harassing her, demanded that they stop, and after an exchange, pushed one of the girls to the ground. Olivia was sent home by the principal, and her parents ended up talking with Sheri.

They were dismayed at the school's decision to punish the wrong child, in their view, and openly expressed pride that their daughter had so courageously stood up for a vulnerable friend.

Sheri asked whether they could foster Olivia's values and courage without supporting behavior that will be harmful and get her in trouble. As much as her parents thought she was a hero, Olivia had injured another child and was in trouble at school, so her heroism didn't accomplish what she might have by taking the high road in terms of tactics. Olivia's parents then saw the gap between their message and how the world was relating to Olivia, and they realized they had more communicating to do with her.

While Olivia's parents empathized with her and appreciated her caring, she needed their guidance to express herself in a way that would allow others to see these aspects, too. They were able to help Olivia understand the concept that *how* she expressed herself needed to carry the same message as *what* she was saying.

In this situation, they explained that speaking up about what she was seeing and then protecting her friend by simply getting her safely away from the other girls—rather than entering the fray with a challenging demand and shove—would have taken care of her friend in a way that contrasted with their unkind behavior. They told Olivia, "When someone does something that goes against your values, it's important to let them know in a way that shows them what your values are."

Be aware of ways you can support your child's character development.

What Others Do and Say Doesn't Define You, It Defines Them

Your identity, motivations, passions, and values are yours to develop, not something constructed by someone else. For example, if somebody calls you a "crybaby," it tells you that they're uncomfortable with tears or with showing feelings. If someone says you're a disappointment, it shows that the person is feeling disappointed. If someone says you're wrong, it means that your response is not the one they agree with or hoped to hear. If someone says you're bad, it means they don't like or approve of your actions or statements.

In each case, the statements others make about you actually tell you something about them. Kids tend to take on disparaging claims and internalize them as true descriptions of themselves; this is where you need to step in and guide your child.

Speaking from your spot, be clear about the message you're sending. Encourage your children to stay on their spot about who they are and to consider that something they said or did may have prompted or contributed to the other person's reaction. That's something they will need to understand and address. But the reaction belongs to that other person, and it's not your child's to internalize and own.

Similarly, encourage your kids to be direct about their feelings and needs rather than framing them as another person's problem in the form of blame or criticism.

As a Parent, You Cannot Legislate Your Child's Values; You Can Only Inspire Them

You can't "instruct" your children about a way to feel or believe and expect them to simply embrace your position, but you can direct their attention, ask them questions, and help them understand and learn for themselves so they build their own internal meaning:

- *"What do you think about what happened?"*
- *"How do you think your friend was feeling? Why might your friend have done that to you?"*
- *"How would you like to handle this?"*

When you get to this last step of helping your child set an action plan with steps to move forward, break it into small parts and be specific about the steps, but don't provide the answers. Help your child walk through it independently, and if things go off track about points you think need to be addressed, direct your child there with questions. Present any suggestions or recommendations and then ask what your child thinks of them, so as to allow your child to maintain ownership of the solution.

Understanding What's at the Heart of the Matter Gives Our Actions Meaning

Sharing the principles that illustrate your values (such as "We care about being good hosts" or "Everyone does their share") to support and explain the rules you ask your kids to follow ("Guests go first" or "Bus your dishes before you leave the table") helps them understand the intentions and heart behind what you are asking of them. When your children grasp how their behaviors affect others, they become stakeholders in your family's values, and those values have meaning to them beyond simply following your rules.

Character Is Always a Work in Progress

Integrity, empathy, inclusion—whatever human qualities you value and want your kids to hold—are not about always getting it right. Character is shaped by experience, and sometimes that experience emerges from the consequences of our thoughtlessness.

Character strength is about being aware of what is going on inside you, knowing what puts you on your spot and pulls you off it, and being willing to care about the effect you have on other people. Character is how you carry yourself as you relate to your world and the people within it, and this, too, constantly evolves and shifts—so missteps are inevitable and necessary for us to grow.

When you recognize this, you can be kinder to yourself about lapses, and when you're kinder to yourself, qualities such as grace, gratitude, forgiveness, and generosity are much easier to tap. And from a kinder place, toward ourselves and our children, it's easier to sort out intentions to have our words and actions line up with the impact we want to have.

The Value of Family Values

The principles and ethics that parents hold are also embedded in the way you run your family. For instance, in families where everyone contributes to meal preparation or clean-up as a reflection of a family value, children come to understand that. They are more likely to become the kids who offer to help or automatically participate when they are guests.

Because family values have a pronounced impact on your children's character, it's important to make your values explicit. Humans are essentially tribal, and most kids appreciate belonging to a group—a family, a cohort, a team, a club, a class—for a variety of reasons, including the sense of connection, inclusion, identity, and camaraderie that "belonging" provides us.

As a result, children are usually very responsive when parents make their values explicit by saying, "In this family, we . . . ," followed by the value you hold and want to demonstrate, because it builds the sense that this family has its own ways of doing things, and that belonging to this family matters.

- *"In this family, we speak kindly to one another."*
- *"In this family, we don't hit or throw things."*
- *"In this family, we each clean up after ourselves."*
- *"In this family, we help one another."*
- *"In this family, we show appreciation when someone does something nice for us."*

With the awareness that your messages impact your children's character development, pay attention to how you organize daily life around what you care about and value, both stated and unstated.

Character Building from Your Spot

It's one thing to parent with "character" when you're on your spot, when things are going well, and when you're confident and in a positive groove with your kids. But it's very different when you're off your spot and overwhelmed, in a bad mood, fed up, off guard, or feeling exposed, inadequate, or defensive. We all get there sometimes, and it can happen with the simplest things in everyday life with kids.

For example, you're giving cookies to your three young children. You have three cookies, and you give one to each of them, then you pour them some milk and feel pretty good about providing a nice treat to the threesome—until somebody says, "Hey, how come *they* get the big ones?"

Suddenly, character issues are on the table, and how you respond is about to give your kids important messages about what matters in life. Do any of these responses sound familiar?

- *"Because you got the bigger cookie last time."* This implies that who gets which size cookie is very important and worth keeping track of, and it reinforces that value with your children. (Remember the waffle chart?)

- *"Too bad, now just be happy with your own cookie!"* This sends an inadvertent message to your kids that compassion doesn't matter when working through a problem.

- *"OK, let me give you some extra chocolate chips to make up for it."* This communicates that avoiding disappointment is a valued strategy and that disappointment earns prompt restitution.

- *"If you complain again, then you get NO cookie!"* This conveys intolerance, and relays an unintended message that disappointment prompts retaliation.

- *"It's not fair? Well, life isn't fair!"* By saying this, you dismiss the "fairness" that you encourage in your family and that you try to model for your children.

So many inadvertent messages to track! No wonder you're exhausted at the end of the day!

In this example, parenting from your spot means remembering to appreciate where your children are coming from with their cookie fairness concern, while holding to the values you want to message to them.

How might you reply to the cookie size complaint, from your spot? If you don't want minor size differences between cookies to be a big deal in your children's lives, you could say something like this:

- *"It just worked out that way this time. Another time it will work out another way. That's just how it is with serving cookies."*

If your kids need to understand more at that point, you can add some insight:

- *"Homemade cookies are each different, so they won't be the exact same size. Homemade cookie eaters need to be able to be good sports about that."*

Be ready to understand that some kids get so caught up in bigger, better, faster, first, or a misunderstanding about "fairness" or "justice" that they may not be able to muster good sportsmanship about a slightly smaller cookie in the moment. Rather than either losing your temper or searching for a larger cookie, let them know, kindly, that the homemade cookie seems to be causing them so much upset right now that they need to take a break and reunite with their cookie later when they can enjoy it as the treat it is meant to be.

Sometimes a cookie is just a cookie, but in instances like this, the cookie itself matters less than the values you're imparting by the way you handle the moment. Countless moments like this go by in a day, and when they do, each one is an opportunity, in real time, to help your kids build character.

Spotlights

- Development of your children's character starts with what they observe about yours.

- How you respond to challenges, disappointments, and the needs of others sends powerful messages to your children.

- Make your values explicit; family values have a huge influence in shaping your children's character—be deliberate about what they learn from you.

- Help your children consider whether their words and actions reflect who they want to be, how they want to act, and what impact they want to have in the world.

- Character development is always a work in progress, and we all have room to learn and grow; model this when you or your children make missteps.

Managing Changes, Small and Big

Change is just what happens in life.

From the moment we wake up in the morning, our lives are shaped by the adjustments we make throughout the day from one task or activity to another, one venue to another, one focus to another, one physical or emotional state to another.

With varying degrees of awareness and ease, our children also manage transition after transition throughout the day. They move from bed to breakfast, car to school, playground to class, out the door, in the door. Our kids shift from following to leading, from absorbing words to expressing words, from remembering to discovering, energized to exhausted—and often, all of this before noon.

Some of our everyday transitions are routine enough to be in the "habit zone." The habit zone is easier and more comfortable for parents and children alike because the shifts happen automatically, usually with less apprehension or drama. Your goal as a parent is to get as many routine shifts as possible into the habit zone.

All parents struggle with preparing kids for transitions, welcome and unwelcome, small and big. The key to managing transitions is to be able to find your spot about each transition, and to make the adjustments needed to stay on your spot as you adapt to change. Staying on your spot as the situation shifts also helps your kids learn to accept changes and make adjustments, because they take their cues from you.

Helping children learn to adapt to everyday changes is also how parents prepare children for the bigger, harder changes life can bring.

Your Everyday Transition IQ

We all have a different capacity to manage and adapt to everyday changes. This capacity is what we refer to as your transition IQ, or "TQ." A parent's TQ is tied to being on their spot, so it can be higher or lower in different everyday transitions.

If transitions are challenging in your family, a good first step is to take inventory of the various transitions in your everyday life with your kids. Make a list of which go smoothly and which are struggles.

Next, look at your smooth transitions and your challenging ones. You'll see patterns emerge. Everyday transitions that go well are typically habitual ones you deem necessary and nonnegotiable. In those situations, you're on your spot so your TQ is high. You clearly communicate when a shift is a suggestion and when it's a requirement. The transitions that are less effective often happen when you are ambivalent, under duress, rushed by time constraints, distracted, or simply not being present in the moment. They happen when you're off your spot so your TQ is low.

One good indicator of how parents manage transitions comes up when kids have a tough time separating, either from parents or from an activity. In these situations, the children are making what is for them a tough adjustment from a want-to activity to a have-to requirement, or from a situation of ease to unease. If you yield to their resistance and delay the transition, or argue while they dig in, you send mixed signals that won't give your children the confident, clear message they need from you to make a shift when it's hard for them.

Transitions go better, for example, when you say, "We're going to put all of our love into one hug and kiss and say goodbye," or clearly say once, "It's time to leave now." Be ready for some disappointment (a feeling that can accompany having to accept an unwanted or unexpected transition).

While some kids may need extra support and encouragement to manage an unwanted change, if you are clear and on your spot about making the shift, it is much more likely to be uneventful, with only minimal and fleeting protests and negotiations.

If you can be consistent about staying on your spot while supporting your children's transitions, your kids will learn to handle changes, too, and they'll develop their own TQ, an important life skill.

What Kids Need from Parents

Everyday transitions are something you usher and orchestrate and oversee, until your children are developmentally ready to manage on their own. There are kids who seem to be adaptable from birth, others who learn to make adjustments at a young age, and those who figure it out when they're older (and for some, making changes persists as a challenge into adulthood). Along the way, how your children learn to deal with everyday transitions depends in large part on the degree of acceptance, grace, and clarity that you bring to each change. For example:

- Is the end of screen time really the end, or time to negotiate how many more minutes your child gets to play games?

- Is "time to leave the house" the time you walk out the door? Or is it time to remind everyone what they need to bring, find misplaced items, hurry the dawdlers, and use the bathroom one last time?

- Is "time to stop playing and get to bed" simply a routine ending for the day, or is it instead time for a routine power struggle?

When you're ambivalent about a transition, the messages you give can be mixed and confusing. Without your clarity, you children are more likely to resist the transition and have a harder time developing the habits that would make it easier for them the next time. When you feel ambivalent about asking you children to make a shift, that is a moment to find your spot. You don't need to choose between what your heart feels and what your judgment says needs to happen. You just need to line them up.

If you are clear that screen time is over, that bedtime is bedtime, and that time to go home is time to go home, you can express your empathy for the disruption as you stand firm about what needs to happen.

- *"I get that you really want to stay online, but now it's time to move on to your chores."*

- *"I love that you have such a good time with your friends in the morning group chat, but we need to leave now. Grab your backpack and tell them you'll see them at school."*

- *"It's bedtime, so let's get ready now."*

Your children look to you to understand how these moments are supposed to work, and how you manage the moments tells them how to respond. The most matter-of-fact transitions for parents are the ones where you are on your spot and clear that the change is something you are on board with. As your conviction—head to toe—comes across to your children, they grow more accepting and matter-of-fact about these transitions.

These are some ways you can build your conviction and increase your TQ:

- **Know yourself and what you need so you can be effective in ushering change.** Since you set the tone for transitions, whenever possible have them happen in a focused yet unemotional and smooth manner. Most parents can't do that when they are distracted, fatigued, or grumpy. Before you initiate a change with your kids, take a moment to focus, find your spot, and get your footing. You need to know where you are and be present before you can guide your kids to whatever is next.

- **Know your children: Take into consideration who they are as you plan for a change that affects them.** Calibrate the time and attention you give to particular transitions with particular kids. Some children have more inertia than others—their bodies at rest stay at rest and their bodies in motion stay in motion. It takes clarity, persistence, and some scaffolding to help kids transition from certain mental states or physical places to another. By staying on your spot, with your full attention and warm yet steady manner guiding them, your children will do better with the transitions.

- **Balance your children's needs around your own.** For example, if you know your child is slow to get to the car because she's the "mayor" of her school campus and likes to say goodbye to everyone on her way to the car, allow enough time for that when you pick her up. If you lose track of time and your computer-immersed kid has to stop her game abruptly to go on a "boring" errand, recognize that since she was unprepared for the transition, she's bound to be unhappy and resistant. Take that into consideration as you respond with empathy, keep your errand on track, and do your best to get everyone's spirits back on track as well.

- **Be aware that schedule shifts like holidays and school breaks can bring myriad changes to family life, some more welcome than others.** Check in with yourself as you organize holiday planning, cooking, hosting, and traveling. Do your best to set things up so that you aren't overextended, overwhelmed, or resentful; this way you can stay on your spot as you navigate the inevitable changes in routine that holidays and school breaks bring. When parents take their own needs and priorities into consideration as they plan for breaks and holidays, it helps optimize this special time with family and friends.

A Tool Kit for Everyday Changes

Here are some pointers to help you handle the transitions that are commonplace in everyday parenting:

1. **Make sure your children know that a planned transition or change is coming.** Since parents are at the helm of how the day goes, little changes are often anticipated by parents but not by kids. Alerting them will help all of you be on the same page.

2. **Make sure kids know what they are moving from and what they are moving to**—for example, from playtime or screen time to homework or dinner. This way, the transition makes sense to them and can become more predictable.

3. **Distinguish have-to transitions from want-to transitions.** Use language that makes it clear whether the change is a **requirement** (*"Time to get ready for bed now"* or *"You have a dentist appointment after school today"*) or an **invitation** (*"Would you like to come have a snack?"* or *"Want to go outside and kick the soccer ball around?"*).

4. **Once you've made transitions or responded to changes, demonstrate encouragement for the shift—even if it wasn't easy.** Whether the kids got settled into the car smoothly or only after a struggle, take a breath and adopt a "now-that-we're here" attitude, forward facing. This allows you to move into the ease and connection you wish had been there in the first place. When parents continue to grumble once the children are finally in the car, at the table, in the bed, or off the screen, it prolongs the tension and reinforces the kids' dread of the transition. Instead, provide a friendly landing that encourages a smoother shift next time.

5. **Review the routine transitions in your daily life, and consider if they can be better organized.** For example, telling children to take a break from homework to have dinner is likely to be an easier transition than asking them to stop a video game to come to the table. Certain transitions go better when they follow less compelling activities rather than highly engaging ones. Sometimes simply reorganizing your routine will make transitions easier.

6. **Allow enough time so that moving from one setting or activity to another is a neutral interaction rather than one fraught with anxiety.** When possible, put enough margins around transitions so you don't create stress. Schedule activities and appointments with enough

gap time so picking your children up from school isn't too much of a rush for them to show you their art project or to interact with a teacher as needed. Ask your kids to stop playing and wash hands for dinner before the hot food is already on the table. Set bedtime so there is ease in that routine rather than interactions fueled by your desperation to make sure they'll get enough sleep.

7. **When you know that events outside of your daily routines are going to happen, give children age-appropriate warning.** These can include anything from doctor appointments to guests coming over, from requesting their help with a yard clean-up to planned vacations. Older kids typically need more warning to plan for the event, and younger children often need a balance of enough warning to be able to anticipate it, but not so much as to become consumed (a birthday several weeks away) or anxious (a vaccination next week).

Change and transitions are indeed just part of our daily lives, and so are "Do I have to?" and "Just five more minutes!" and "You didn't tell me!" and "No, I'm not . . . going/coming/stopping/doing!" Be understanding and treat these kinds of reactions to change as simply a first response to an unwanted shift, rather than an all-out refusal, which positions you for a power struggle.

Being understanding as you manage changes and transitions helps you more effectively consider your reactions. Acknowledge that it's not what they want to do, let them know kindly but firmly that it's one of those have-tos, give them the amount of support that their age or state of mind requires, and manage the moment as just a moment.

Once on the other side of a difficult transition with your child, take a breath, let go of the annoyance, find your spot, and move into whatever is next—a goodbye at the door, a good-night kiss, dinnertime—with heart for both of you.

Dealing with Unexpected, Bigger Changes

Big changes in life sometimes follow the choices we make, or they may be caused by circumstances out of our control. Both types of these big changes can be hard adjustments for children and adults, even the joyful ones like a new baby, and especially the sorrowful ones, like a loved one's death.

Most big changes are unpredictable for kids, even if they're anticipated by their parents: relocating to a new home and neighborhood, parents separating or divorcing, a best friend moving far away, or a pet dying. Some of these big changes may be unpredictable to parents, too, and everyone may be thrown off-balance when patterns of life and emotional well-being are disrupted. Big changes can dramatically disrupt family life and impact each family member.

It's difficult to position parents for the gravity, disturbance, and pain of sudden, tragic events in a single short chapter, much less help prepare you for the challenge of recovering from a life-altering experience as you're trying to regain more familiar rhythms of life. However, your everyday parenting that equips and supports your kids through small changes and builds their TQ will also help give them the confidence, resilience, and hope to manage the significant changes that happen in their lives.

What children also need when there are big, difficult changes are assurances that even when grown-ups are upset, they are still there to hold and support their kids. And as we all do in a crisis, children need opportunities to feel secure and cared for to offset their feelings of helplessness. When life as they've known it has shifted on them, your communication with your children needs to be especially thoughtful and clear.

Here is some guidance for parenting from your spot during big changes and challenging transitions.

1. **When big changes throw you off-balance, your kids need to know that though you may stumble, you can be counted on to take care of them (or that you'll make sure that someone else will).** Do your best to keep their familiar routines and patterns intact. If you are unsettled, scared, pained, or grieving, make sure to convey that you are having big feelings that may temporarily affect your behavior and availability, but that you are still you, and you are still there for them, and things will come back to "normal" (albeit perhaps a "new normal") in time.

2. **It's okay to ask for support from your children.** You may need extra cooperation, additional space, or greater understanding; you may need them to temporarily be more self-sufficient. Let them know you believe they can rise to the occasion, and count on their compassion and caring. Your overt appreciation and confidence in your children will comfort them. When something out of control and upsetting happens, it helps for kids (and adults) to be able to "do" something that makes a difference. It reminds us that there is agency in how we deal with things, even if we can't influence what is happening.

3. **Let your children tell others what's happening so they can be the ones to share the news, when appropriate.** If something serious happens in your family, for example, let your kids convey the situation to their teachers, neighbors, and friends. You can stand by with clarifications as needed. The process of telling what happened provides another opportunity for kids to experience some agency: *"I can tell the story. I can carry and give information. I can take an active role in a conversation about this by providing some details and observations."* This helps kids relate to and accept changes and contributes to healing.

4. **Be thoughtful about having adult conversations around kids and flooding them with more information than they need or can handle.** Keep conversations with kids age-appropriate so they can hear and understand them.

5. **Tell children what you know and what you don't know about the changes.** For example: *"Mom and I will be living apart for a while. I don't know how long, but I do know that I'll be seeing you a lot. We know that I will be moving to a different place in the next week or two. I'm not sure where I'll be staying, but I know it will definitely be nearby. We don't know the schedule yet, but you'll be spending time with both of us."*

6. **Be sure to take care of yourself.** Whether you're feeling sturdy or not, your children will turn to you to gauge stability. Addressing your own needs will help you be able to assure and steady them.

Changes small and big are what happen to all of us on our path through life. You can support your children through transitions by helping them understand that while you can't guarantee constancy in life, they can count on your strength and commitment to do your best to be there for them when they need you. You can empower them daily by expressing (through both words and manner) your confidence in their resilience and adaptability. If they come to believe they can manage and get through what life presents, then changes—small and big—will be something they know they can handle.

Spotlights

- Stay on your spot so everyday shifts will be routine transitions rather than routine power struggles.

- When helping children adjust to changes, remind them of what you do know and what you don't know (yet) so they can adjust to what's next.

- When parents help kids manage everyday changes, children are prepared to handle the bigger, harder ones that come their way.

- When difficult changes unsettle your family, your sturdiness will reassure your kids; tend to your own needs to better support theirs.

- Empower your kids by expressing confidence in their adaptability so they know they can manage changes—small and big.

CHAPTER 14

Parenting in the Home Stretch: It's Never Too Late

It's never too late for you to make a positive difference in your kids' lives and in your relationship with them.

Conventional parenting wisdom holds that children begin to pull back from their parents starting in the middle school years, as kids' attention shifts more to their peers and they seek to differentiate themselves from you. It's true that your children will press to become more independent; that's natural because it's your kids' job to become self-sufficient, and that means gradually separating from their parents.

Often parents assume that as their children rely less on them, their influence and importance in their kids' lives will diminish from this point forward. As kids get older, parents may believe they are less able to affect their relationships with their children, and feel that they've "missed the boat."

This is not true. Your relationship with your child is not a boat that can be missed. It's a boat you're on together, and it's never too late to navigate in a new or different direction.

It's never too late to show your support for your kids to guide them when they need it, and to strengthen your bond with them.

Build on the Positives

Pause and reflect on what you do well as a parent. Make note of the areas of your relationship that feel good and work well, and also identify those areas that still need attention.

In the home stretch and beyond, there are always things you can do to strengthen and solidify your relationship with your kids so that your connection remains strong after they are launched. The key, now, is building on the positives.

Be sure you let your children know how much you appreciate it when they confide in you, relate respectfully, are good hosts and guests, take on responsibilities, and show compassion and caring. Communicate how much it contributes to the well-being of your family and the positive impact it has on you and others.

Make certain you reflect the way the world works by connecting freedom and privileges according to the trust they've earned—for instance, "Thanks for volunteering to drive your little brother to his game, and for gassing up the car today. You're welcome to use the car to meet up with your friends this weekend."

At any stage, when your children are open and straightforward with you and bring up issues to discuss, be sure to share your appreciation and tell them how important that is to you. Build on the positives by showing that you are grateful for their honesty and candor, especially when it isn't easy to own up to something—for example, "I'm sorry that happened, but I really appreciate that you let me know. It means a lot to me that I can count on you to be honest and open." If you haven't expressed that enough to your children, you can begin now.

When your primary focus is on the relationship with your kids, your gratitude for your child's honesty and openness comes through first; addressing the issue comes next. This dynamic makes it safe for your kids to be honest. When parents get so triggered by their child's disclosure that they become upset and judgmental, kids regret having been honest and figure it would be better to find ways to avoid your reaction in the future. That's an inadvertent message you don't want to send.

When your children overcome setbacks, acknowledge their character, strengths, and resilience. Most disappointments kids experience are fleeting, unless we adults layer on our own emotions and turn the moments into events. When your older kids demonstrate resilience, it's worthy of acknowledgment because it shows they're getting the message that being able to make the best of whatever happens is a key to their well-being. For example, "I know how much you wanted to be in the starting lineup, and I'm so proud of you for how well you got past your feelings and rooted for your teammates" or "We appreciate how well you handled it when we had to cancel our trip at the last minute. We're so proud of you for understanding and for figuring out a fun summer for yourself."

It's common for parents to focus on what's not working with kids and take for granted those things that are, and this is especially true with our older children. So notice that and remember to reinforce and appreciate what's going well. Tell kids what you value in them, and why. Build on the positives about who they are and how they approach their relationships and lives. This will inform the self-image they bring forward.

Shaping Skills for Being Out in the World

Just as home is the training ground for helping young kids learn how to manage in the world outside of home, it's also the training ground to help older kids learn to manage in the world when they leave home.

This makes the home stretch the time to think about additional life skills your kids will need when they're on their own. Help them understand what you'll continue to do for them and what they need to be able to do for themselves. When you provide your children with opportunities to gain necessary life skills while they're with you, you're able to influence the competence and values they bring to those abilities when they are on their own.

As kids grow and are able to take on more responsibilities, it's helpful to tie those responsibilities at each stage of development to skills they can use as they navigate life outside of your household. The home stretch is a good time to evaluate and shift chores and roles so that your almost-launched kids build the essential skills they'll need to operate independently. Think about what your children need to be able to do on their own, and prioritize those things.

For example, doing the laundry, cleaning the bathroom, or cooking simple meals are all good chores to shift to when it comes to skill-building for a young person about to leave home. If you're still waking your kids up and getting them moving, now is the time to introduce an alarm. It's OK to let them be late a couple of times now, rather than having to learn the hard way after they leave home and the stakes get higher.

If they aren't already pitching in at home without being asked, teach your kids to become aware of what's happening around them and how to offer help on their own. Show them how to watch for cues. When you get home from the grocery store, they can initiate helping carry the bags in. If you are entertaining guests, they can assist you with preparation and clean-up. If there are dirty dishes in the sink, they can begin to take notice and wash them. This is a time when being a conscientious family member prepares kids to be an appreciated roommate. Be sure to show your gratitude so they understand that these gestures make a difference.

How they manage money, set up a doctor's appointment, shop for food and essentials—these are more of the life skills they will need. Give your children a head start to develop these skills while you're there to guide them.

Keep Your Eye on Your Lifelong Relationship

Most of us don't think much about the home stretch when our kids are younger. Everyday life is so all-consuming and hands-on, it's often hard to imagine what's coming beyond a single parenting moment, let alone a given day, week, or school year. Over time you build your relationship with your children, supporting their developing capacities and independence along the way; and then, before you know it, the moment to send them off into the world is right in front of you!

For some parents, this is when they recognize what their children still need to learn (like certain manners), do (like cleaning up after themselves), and know (like how to manage their schedules) to be ready to leave home. It's a wake-up call about the parenting roles you still have, the ones they've outgrown, and the ones they tell you they've outgrown but really still need your help with. As you take stock of your relationship with your kids and their readiness to leave home, you may wonder if you missed your chance to be the parent you hoped to be.

Know that it is never too late to . . .

- find your spot as a parent, and begin to relate from there.
- create the kind of relationship you want with your children.
- make your family life one that supports your kids to thrive in the world.
- begin setting limits with your kids.
- change communication patterns at home to more positive ones that encourage your children's social skills and relationships
- help your kids build true self-esteem, balancing their self-care with care for others.
- strengthen your children's disappointment muscles and to learn to flex your own.
- learn about your kids' online lives, to get to know that part of their world better and to address balancing life on and off screens.
- infuse your values into your interactions with your kids so they understand the impact they can have on their world.

As your kids grow and become more independent and capable, you step back, but you don't step away.

Ultimately, parenting from your spot across your children's first eighteen years lays the foundation for a lifelong relationship with them. What you hope for, after all, is that once they're off in the world and no longer dependent on you, your kids will still want you to be part of their life, and they'll want to be part of yours. So as you move through the years, including the home stretch and beyond, take every opportunity to keep communication open and to strengthen your bond with your kids. It's never too late.

Acknowledgments

We are incredibly grateful to a skilled and generous cohort of editors, advisors, and supporters who helped us create *Raising Kids*.

We were blessed when Matt Holt recognized the book's potential and enthusiastically brought us into BenBella's family, supported by the extraordinary talent of an amazing publication team, especially Katie Dickman, Karen Wise, Kim Broderick, Mallory Hyde, Kerri Stebbins, and Brigid Pearson.

We deeply appreciate the unrelenting support of Soren Kaplan, whose creative advice and tremendous encouragement repeatedly helped us leapfrog our obstacles.

Thanks again to Felicia Eth, whose tenacious commitment to our book combined with her editorial wisdom was a huge source of inspiration. We're also indebted to the guidance and encouragement of Bonnie Nadell and Andy Ross, who generously shared their advice to help us shape our book and pointed us in the right direction.

We're grateful to Vikki Bowes-Mok and Tanya Jorgenson, our earliest editors, who carved a canoe out of a tree trunk; and to Laura Konigsberg and Karen Craigo, our latter-stage editors, who set us on course down the river. And with special appreciation for the care and countless hours Lauren Gaylord and Vik devoted to the final round of editing; you turned the canoe into a speedboat.

Acknowledgments

We thank Julie Lythcott-Haims for believing in our project; we hope our work supports hers, and we are honored to have her foreword helping propel this book.

Thanks to our other editorial advisors and influencers, whose insights about the book, the publishing world, and marketing positioned and then repositioned our thinking, keeping us on course: Alison Inches, Karen Eisenberg, Rebecca Hunt, and Larkin Page-Jacobs.

To all of these incredible friends and supporters and many more unnamed here, thank you most of all for believing in the importance of this book, and for the enthusiasm you shared that motivated us when we needed it. As a result of your faith in this project, parents everywhere now have this guide to turn to for help as they find their way—and find their spot—raising kids.

Index

Index

B

balance
and being on your spot, 9
of child's and your needs, 169
in digital life, 149–151
for social development, 90
of want-tos and have-tos, 35, 153,
166–167
of work and family life, 142, 153
bedtime
being off your spot on, 13–14
child's point of view on, 27–28
and homework, 13, 14, 136
inadvertent messages about, 46
limit setting related to, 75
technology use at, 147
transition at, 167, 168
behavior(s). *see also* misbehavior; *specific
types*
communication about, 42–43
and feelings, 62–64
at home vs. school, 122–123,
128–129
inadvertent messages in, 46
influence of your, 33–34
labeling children's, 89, 107, 158–159
linking outcome to, 47–48
making sense of child's, 73–74
being on your child's side, 5–6, 16, 29, 30,
53, 71, 80, 130
belonging, sense of, 108, 111, 161
the best, being or having, 110, 155–156
blame, 94, 99, 159
boundary maintenance
and over-/under-identifying with child,
26
related to screen time, 150–151
between school life and homelife,
131–133
and self-esteem, 111
during social interactions, 88–89
to teach self-regulation, 68
on technology use, 147–148
boundary pushing, 6, 126
boundary setting. *see also* limit setting
clear communication about, 51
for communication, 40
in digital life, 144–146
to support social development, 90
bribes, 70, 80

C

car
fighting in, 30
seat belt use in, 10–11
technology use in, 148–149
caring, 157–158
cause-and-effect relationships, 47–48, 51
celebrating common milestones, 108
change
encouraging, 168, 170
as natural part of life, 165
right-sized feelings about, 59–60
in social interactions, 91
unexpected, 171–174
change management, 165–174
in everyday transitions, 167–171
helping children learn, 167–169
tool kit for, 169–171
in unexpected, bigger changes, 171–174
your transition IQ, 166–167
character development, 153–164
and family values, 161
finding your spot on issues related to,
161–163
messages that support, 157–160
your influence on, 153–156
charts, 69–70
citizenship, 126
clarity
in communication, 50–53, 167–168
in limit setting, 76–77
on safety issues, 10–11
clean-up time, 15
commitment, to safety issues, 10–11
commonalities, celebrating, 108
communication, 39–54
about big, unexpected changes, 173
about transitions, 166–168
with adolescents, 92, 102, 176, 179
building on what works in, 53
to clarify roles, requests, and
requirements, 50–51
connection in, 24, 52–53, 73, 75
digital, 144–146
empathy in, 41–42
firm, 15, 40, 42, 78
honest, 48–49, 145–146, 173, 176–177
inadvertent vs. deliberate messages in,
40, 43–46
managing, in the moment, 42–43

Index

Index

outcomes
  communication focused on, 22–23
  consequences vs., 79–81
  linking behaviors to, 47–48
over-identification, with child, 13, 25–26, 57
overinvolvement, avoiding. *see* right-sized involvement
over-sensitivity, 114–115
overwhelmed, feeling, 5. *see also* off your spot, being

P

parent–child relationship
  in adolescence, 175–176, 179
  being on your spot as extension of, 12
  communication focused on, 22–23
  demonstrating social skills in, 94
  and digital life, 144
  lifelong, 178–180
  messages that are mindful of, 21–22
  strengthening, 6 (*see also* relationship building)
parenting. *see also specific topics*
  adversarial approach to, 6, 71, 80–81
  confidence in, 6–7, 118
  in everyday situations, 3–5
  flexibility in, 19–20
  formulaic methods for, 2–3
  in home stretch (*see* adolescents)
  lessons from parents on, 3–4
  patterns in, 6
  professional training in, 4
  relationship-based, 3, 6, 21–22, 48
  top-down, 27
  in unexpected situations, 19–20
  universal aspects of, 3–5
parents
  lessons on parenting from, 3–4
  as prototype for "others," 34
  relationship between, 30, 31
patterns. *see also* rituals; routines
  of homelife, 34–36
  limiting setting to establish, 74–75
  in parenting, 6
  victim and villain, 98–99
peer relationships, 30, 90. *see also* friends and friendships
perspective, maintaining. *see also* right-sized involvement
  in communication, 42–43

in social interactions, 90, 93, 103
phone, checking, 147
physical activity, 150
physical safety, 10–11, 35
planned transitions, preparing for, 169, 170
point of view, child's
  discussing, with teachers, 130
  examining behavior from, 73–74
  relationship building by seeing, 27–28
  understanding feelings from, 57
policies, family
  for adolescents, 74
  on technology use, 147–149
popularity, 101–102
positives, building on, 5, 53, 176–177
power struggles
  and being on your spot, 1–2
  limit setting to work through, 77–79
  messaging during, 47
  over screen time, 149, 151
  relationship building to avoid, 27–28
  during transitions, 171
praise, 106
presence. *see* spot, being on your
privacy, online, 145–146
privileges, for adolescents, 176
progress, in character development, 160–161
protect, urge to
  children's, 157–158
  inadvertent messages/actions due to, 44, 46
  resisting, to build resilience, 113
  and setting limits, 72
  in social interactions, 88
psychological safety, 39, 48–49
punishment
  communication focusing on, 22
  consequences framed as, 79–81
  and limit setting, 71
  making it right vs. delivering, 82
  and technology use, 145–146
pushback, from children, 41–42

R

reciprocity, 96, 122, 126
relating to your child
  in adolescence, 179
  communication for, 23–24
  in digital world, 142–144
  and social interactions, 87–88

Index

About the Authors

Sheri Glucoft Wong, LCSW, is a San Francisco Bay Area family therapist and parenting expert who counsels and speaks to hundreds of parents every year, both in her own practice and at private and public schools, medical and mental health centers, law firms, businesses, nonprofits, and religious organizations across California. She served as the resident parenting coach for Apple, Gymboree, and Genentech, and has trained health care professionals at the Stanford Medical Center and UCSF Benioff Children's Hospital. Sheri lectures at universities including Stanford, UC Berkeley, and UC San Francisco, consulted with faculty at Yale Center for Emotional Intelligence, and was a featured speaker at the "Pediatrics in the Pandemic Age" national conference for pediatricians. Her parenting advice has been showcased in the media, including KTVU television in San Francisco, the *Wall Street Journal*, the *San Francisco Chronicle*, and HuffPost. Sheri completed a national satellite media tour across the country on best parenting practices that reached over 2 million viewers.

Dr. Olaf "Ole" Jorgenson is a school leader and teacher who has supported parents at public and private schools across the western United States as well as in Asia, Europe, and Central America. Ole is head of school at Almaden Country Day School in San Jose, California, serving 385 children in preschool through eighth grade. Ole works closely with parents on a daily basis and is attuned to the prevailing needs, anxieties, and concerns challenging them today, especially in Silicon Valley's fast-paced environment. Ole speaks and publishes widely in education, including dozens of conference presentations and journal articles and three previous books, across a range of subjects in education and educational leadership. He is a field instructor for the Klingenstein Center for Independent and International School Leadership at Teachers College, Columbia University, where he also serves on the Center's advisory board. Ole's parenting expertise was included in the *New York Times* bestselling parenting book, *How to Raise an Adult: Break Free from the Overparenting Trap and Prepare your Kid for Success* by Julie Lythcott-Haims.